Angela Hewitt's keen interest in food and cooking dates back to early childhood. She is a self-taught cook and has run her own catering business on the Isle of Wight for almost twenty years. Her own restaurant, 'Lugleys', opened in 1980. It was an instant success and she soon found her cooking recommended in all the top Good Food Guides, internationally as well as nationally. In her last year she won a special award for her exceptional puddings.

In 1992 she gave up the practical side of catering to develop her career in writing.

Although a lover of every kind of food she has a strong interest in British regional and seasonal cooking. Particularly English fruits, wild food and game. She believes British recipes are amongst the best in the world; especially now that they have been enhanced by the lighter touches modern tastes call for.

Angela is a keen traveller and her first cookery book *Cooking on the Move* was written for the tourist who prefers caravan and boating holidays.

Writing *Isle of Wight Cookery* was a special pleasure for Angela as the Island has provided her with a wonderful home for the past twenty-four years. She lives in Whippingham with her husband and dog.

ISLE OF WIGHT COOKERY

ANGELA HEWITT

Drawings by Louise Dobbs

THE DOVECOTE PRESS LTD

To Beverly and Janet

First published in 1994 by The Dovecote Press Ltd
Stanbridge, Wimborne, Dorset BH21 4JD

ISBN 1 874336 23 7

© Angela Hewitt 1994

Phototypeset by The Typesetting Bureau
Wimborne, Dorset
Printed and bound by Biddles Ltd
Guildford and Kings Lynn

CONTENTS

INTRODUCTION

First and foremost I'm a gourmet and chef, so when I set out to gather together the recipes for this book I was determined that the ones I chose should be enjoyable to eat. Dipping into the past in search of traditional recipes, it immediately struck me that most wouldn't suit today's palate: indeed some recipes such as mackerel boiled in brine would be positively inedible!

In addition, many new ingredients have been introduced to us over the past thirty years or so. Much old-fashioned traditional cooking, with a few honourable exceptions, would now taste extremely bland. Hopefully this book will redress the balance.

If spectacular recipes don't abound, then the marvellous food produced by the Island's micro-climate more than compensates. *Isle of Wight Cookery* is a celebration of an 'Island Retreat' dedicated to self-sufficiency, market gardening and good wholesome eating – where the quality of food speaks for itself.

The Isle of Wight is small, a mere 94,000 acres of varied soils. The landscape, which includes open downland, intimate valleys, lush grazing land and broad-leaved forests, is as diverse and rich in natural beauty as anywhere in England. For at least the last two centuries it has been known as the 'Garden of England'. Its greatest blessing is its protected position off the Southern coast, which has given it a mild temperate climate. Extremes are rare, and snow seldom settles, even on its highest hills.

The mild winters and extended summers give the Island's farmers and market-gardeners a lengthier growing season than many other parts of the country. We can, for instance, enjoy sweet fresh strawberries from as early as May to as late as November. The arable soils of the Arreton Valley in the centre of the Island have long been famous for their fertility, as good for barley and sheep as they are for asparagus and strawberries.

There's also no shortage of food to be harvested from the seas round the Island's coast, including sea bass, plaice, mackerel and herring. Shellfish are a particular speciality of the Island, and both crab and lobster lunches are easy to find in many of the pubs, restaurants and cafes. And for those with a thirst, there are the wines from three vineyards, an Island brewed beer, our own bottled water, as well as apple juice and fruit wines.

This sense of self-sufficiency undoubtedly owes its origins to the Island's insularity. Today, many innovative locals have set-up splendid businesses based on food, offering first class 'home-made' style produce, from ice-cream to smoked salmon, cheese biscuits to oysters.

Perhaps the greatest success has been that of a once uncommon bulb, garlic. Thanks to the Boswell family the Island is now firmly on the international agricultural map, for much of their crop ends up in garlic-loving France. Its pungent aroma seasons the air in Arreton Valley, and every August, at the annual Garlic Festival, up to thirty thousand people gather to sample such delights as ice-cream, lager, mushrooms and prawns – all of them flavoured with garlic.

The growing season on the Island never seems to stop, and as one year of plenty rolls into another, the demand for the Island's produce becomes greater than ever.

Perhaps more importantly, the Island has long been considered a holiday resort and it has been a tradition for inns and tea-shops to provide sustenance for its many visitors. Many premises had their own baker's ovens and produced a variety of small cakes, particularly the popular 'Isle of Wight Dough-nut'. The popularity of the afternoon tea has grown, and many establishments offering good home-cooking are open throughout the year.

The recipes in this book have been chosen to reflect the splendid and prolific raw materials available to Islanders and the Island's many chefs. Because of the quality of produce simple recipes have proven to be best, and traditional recipes have been rewritten with modern tastes in mind.

ANGELA HEWITT
Cowes

SOUPS AND STARTERS

Garlic, Potato and White Wine Soup

Isle of Wight garlic is internationally renowned, and this silky, smooth, cream soup, slightly sweetened by the wine, does it great justice. Serve piping hot with garlic and parsley croutons. A must for any autumn dinner party.

1 lb (450 gm) potatoes
2 large onions
½ pt (275 ml) dry or medium white wine
10-12 skinned garlic cloves
1 pt (570 ml) vegetable or chicken stock
oil for frying
2 tbsp fresh chopped parsley
salt and black pepper
soured cream and paprika to garnish

Finely slice the onions. Peel and dice the potatoes. Put the onion and potato in a heavy bottomed saucepan with the garlic and about 4 tbsp oil. Cover with a lid and simmer very gently, until the vegetables are soft and mushy. It is essential that the vegetables don't brown. Add the wine and stock and simmer for 20 minutes. Purée the contents of the pan to a smooth consistency. Check seasoning. Add the parsley if using. Reheat and serve garnished with the soured cream and paprika, and garlic croutons. If the consistency is too thick add a drop more stock or wine. Serves 4.

Garlic Croutons

Cut a stale French stick into thin ¼ inch slices. Place on a baking sheet in a low temperature oven to dry out. In a processor blend together 2 cloves of garlic, 2 tbsp of olive oil and a large bunch of fresh parsley. Spoon this sauce on top of the crisp croutons and arrange on top of the soup with the dollops of soured cream.

Mussels and Bacon in Garlic, Parsley and Lemon Butter

Mussels are readily available all year round on the Island. If you double up the portions this recipe will make a substantial luncheon dish. Serve with masses of crusty bread to mop up the delicious buttery juices. I often serve in an upturned brioche, split open, so that the mussels appear to be tumbling out of a shell.

2 lb (1 kilo) fresh mussels
1 lb (450 gm) smoked streaky bacon
4 cloves garlic
4 oz (110 gm) butter
½ oz (10 gm) fresh chopped parsley
juice of half a lemon
4 tbsp white wine

Thoroughly scrub the mussels and remove the wiry black beards. Put them in a large heavy-bottomed saucepan and tightly seal on the lid. Place over a high heat for 3 minutes. Remove lid and take out any of the shells that have opened. As you are doing this more shells will begin to open. Continue removing until all the opened shells are out of the saucepan. Discard any that after 8-10 minutes have refused to open. Remove the mussels from the shells and cool. De-rind the bacon and cut each rasher in half. Wrap around the mussels. If the mussels are small use two per piece of bacon. Put to one side until ready to grill.

Mix together the butter, chopped parsley and crushed garlic cloves. Put the mussels and bacon in a deepish grill pan. Dot with half the garlic butter. Place under a hot grill and cook until the bacon is turning a crispy golden colour. (This dish can also be oven baked for 10-15 minutes on high).

Transfer to the hob. Add the remaining butter, the

11

lemon juice and white wine. Raise the heat and shake the pan around until the liquid has reduced, and a thick homogenised sauce has developed. Serve in soup plates or rustic type bowls. Serves 4.

Mushrooms in Garlic and Tarragon Sauce

I like to make this dish in late summer, when it's possible to get local wild mushrooms. Garlic mushrooms have become very popular, particularly as pub grub. This recipe is made more stylish with the addition of cream and tarragon.

1 lb (450 gm) button mushrooms
small packet of fresh tarragon
8 cloves of garlic, skinned
¼ pt (150 ml) white wine or dry sherry
1 pt (570 ml) whipping or double cream
salt and black pepper
oil for frying

Wipe the mushrooms clean (keep them dry). Gently heat the oil in a pan large enough to hold all the mushrooms. Add the mushrooms and sâuté until they begin to turn a pale golden colour. Meanwhile put the garlic cloves in cold water. Bring to the boil, simmer for 10 minutes then drain. Discard the water. To the mushrooms add the white wine. Simmer for one minute, then add the cream, chopped tarragon, tender garlic cloves and seasoning. Simmer until the sauce begins to thicken. Serve in earthenware bowls with French crusty bread. Serves 4.

Garlic and Red Wine Jelly

A real test for true garlic addicts. Delicious served with crisp salad leaves dressed in good quality olive oil and Salsa Verdi. Also good with thick slices of home-baked ham.

1 sachet aspic crystals
12 oz (350 gm) plump garlic cloves
1 large red pepper, finely diced
1 oz (25 gm) fresh chopped parsley
olive oil, ¼ pt (150 ml) red wine
1 tbsp red wine vinegar

Remove the papery skins from the cloves. Put the cloves in a saucepan of cold water and bring to the boil. Drain. Cover with fresh cold water and repeat. Do this three times in total. The last time continue simmering until the cloves are tender. Soften the diced pepper in the olive oil. In a 1 pt (570 ml) terrine layer the garlic, the pepper and the parsley until all used up. Make up the aspic crystals according to the instructions but substituting a ¼ pt (150 ml) of water with the red wine. Add the vinegar. Pour into the terrine and refrigerate until set.

To serve: cut into thick wedges and garnish with the Salsa Verdi. Serves 4.

Salsa Verdi
1 oz (25 gm) fresh parsley
3 or 4 cloves of garlic
1 tbsp capers
1 small tin anchovies
¼ pt (150 ml) olive oil

Briefly rinse the anchovies under cold water. Put in a blender with the rest of the ingredients. Whiz until smooth.

Potted Lobster

Unfortunately, lobster doesn't go very far. Approximately 7 oz (200 gm) of meat comes from a 1 lb (450 gm) lobster. Because of this most recipes are designed to make a little go a long way.

Potted lobster is rich and full of spices, only small portions are necessary. (Crab and prawns can be given the same treatment).

1½ lb (650 gm) cooked lobster
1 thick slice of fresh lemon
6 oz (175 gm) butter
¼ pt (150 ml) white wine
¼ tspn each of ground black pepper, cayenne pepper,
nutmeg, mace and salt to taste

Gently melt the butter with all the spices and the lemon slice in a large frying pan. Add the wine. Raise the heat and bubble the mixture until the wine has almost evaporated. Remove the lemon slice. Extract the lobster meat and roe from the shell, dice and add to the buttery sauce. Simmer very gently for 1-2 minutes until the meat is heated through (don't overcook). Spoon the lobster mixture into 4 ramekin dishes, along with all the flavoursome butter and juices. Cool, then refrigerate until ready to serve. Serve at room temperature with a salad garnish and brown or country bread. Serves 4.

Lobster Jelly

Every time I make this dish I think of heaven; for this must surely be the sort of food they serve there.

one 2 lb (900 gm) live lobster
½ pt (275 ml) white wine
1 celery stick, washed
1 carrot, washed
1 leek, washed
3 or 4 fennel seeds
dill or fennel leaves for garnish
1 tbsp lemon juice
½ sachet or 4 leaves of gelatine to set ½ pt (275 ml) liquid
6 tbsp whipped double cream
1 tbsp mayonnaise
¼ peeled and finely diced cucumber

Boil the lobster in 2 pt (1.1 lt) water for 12 minutes, then shell. Reserve water and shells. To the water, add the vegetables, white wine, shells and fennel seeds. Simmer for about half an hour until the liquid is reduced to about ½ pt (275 ml). Strain to remove vegetables etc. Dissolve the gelatine crystals in 2 tbsp cold water or soften the leaf gelatine in cold water and add to the hot stock with the lemon juice. Slice the tail meat into medallions, and chop the claw and leg meat. Divide this meat between four moulds, reserving the meat from one of the legs and claws. Pour the jellied stock into the moulds to cover the meat then refrigerate until set. If wished a sprig of fennel or dill can be set in the jelly with the lobster meat.

Finely chop the reserved lobster meat and mix with the mayonnaise, whipped cream and cucumber. Season.

To serve, turn out the jellied lobster and garnish with the fennel or dill leaves and a scoop of lobster cream. Serves 4.

ASPARAGUS

This princely vegetable has a flavour few others can hope to compete with. It is rarely served as an accompanying vegetable as it is much too special.

Asparagus growing is for the patient gardener prepared to wait several years for the asparagus bed to strengthen and prosper. The first year's harvest of spindly spears should be left untouched. The second year a few bunches can be collected, and a few more the third year. The first real harvest is in the fourth year and every year after that providing you treat your asparagus bed well, and keep on enriching it with fertilizer and compost.

Forget special asparagus pots, they're totally useless. The best way to cook them is to fill a large pan with water, choosing one wide enough to take the spears on their side. Bring the water to the boil, add the spears and boil for about 8 minutes, depending how thick they are. Scoop out with a fish slice and drain flat on a wire rack.

To prepare for cooking cut off the woody base. This is done by trial and error, but you'll soon get the hang of it. For a professional effect remove the fine skin from the thickest part with a potato peeler.

The best asparagus is the freshest, ideally picking and eating on the same day. It soon looses its crispness, and the stems start to look shrivelled on old asparagus.

Feuillet of Asparagus with Mint Bernaise Sauce

8 oz (225 gm) puff pastry
1 lb (450 gm) asparagus, 1 shallot
¼ pt (150 ml) white wine, 2 tbsp white wine vinegar
1 tbsp fresh chopped mint, 2 large egg yolks
4 oz (110 gm) best butter, cut into cubes

Roll the puff pastry into a rectangle 8 inches long and 4 inches wide. Then cut across the width into four oblongs. Place on a baking tray. Coat with egg wash and score a pattern on the surface with a fork. Bake in a hot oven 425f/220c/gas 7 for 10 minutes, or until golden in colour. Remove from the oven and cool until ready to use.

Remove the woody bases from the asparagus and with a potato peeler remove the stringy outer skin. Fill a pan, large enough to take the asparagus lying down, with water. Add the asparagus, bring to the boil and simmer for 5 minutes until tender but not too soft. The spears should remain firm and not become floppy.

Meanwhile make the sauce. Place a basin over a saucepan of boiling water. In the basin put the shallot, the wine and the vinegar, heat through. Add the egg yolks and whisk until thick and foamy, and gently heated through. Add the chopped mint then slowly beat in the cubed butter until all used up and a rich sauce has formed. If the sauce is too thick add a tiny drop of wine. It is essential you don't over-heat the sauce or it will separate.

To serve, heat the puff pastry oblongs through, split open and arrange the drained asparagus on the bottom half. Pour over the minty Bernaise, and arrange the remaining piece of pastry on the top. Garnish with a fresh sprig of mint. Serves 4.

Royal Asparagus Soup

Avoid the cheaper, thin, spindly stems sometimes on offer. It might seem a good idea if you only want to make soup. But remember asparagus soup must be sieved to eradicate the stringy skins. The poorer the grade of asparagus the more stringy it will be.

1½ lb (700 gm) medium quality asparagus
2 small onions
1 small clove of garlic
1½ pt (900 ml) good chicken or vegetable stock
2 oz (50 gm) butter
1 tbsp oil
¼ pt (150 ml) single cream
salt and pepper

Finely slice the onions. Cut the asparagus into short lengths, and reserve the spear heads. In a saucepan put the butter, oil, onion, garlic and cut asparagus. Put over a low heat and cover the saucepan. Stew very gently until the vegetables are soft and pulpy. Add the stock and bring to the boil. Strain through a sieve and reserve the stock. Put the vegetables in a processor and blend until smooth. Push this purée through a sieve or mouli. Add to the stock. Season to taste and add the cream and asparagus tips. Simmer the soup until the tips are tender and serve. Garnish with a dollop of whipped or soured cream. Serves 4.

Asparagus and Quail's Egg Salad

In this salad the asparagus is still warm, an excellent compromise if undecided on whether to serve a hot or a cold starter.

1 lb (450 gm) best quality asparagus
8 quails' eggs
8 thin slices of one day old, French bread
12 black olives
4 sun-dried tomatoes in oil
8 walnut halves, coarsely chopped
4 tbsp salad oil (I like grapeseed oil for this dish)
1 tbsp balsamic vinegar
1 curly endive or other crisp lettuce

Wash the curly endive or lettuce and divide between four plates. Make the salad dressing; chop the sun dried tomatoes and mix with the walnuts, salad oil and vinegar. Lightly toast the bread and spread with butter. Divide the toast around the four plates. Remove the woody ends and stringy skin from the asparagus, then cook for 6 minutes in a pan of boiling water. Drain the asparagus and pour the dressing over. Meanwhile bring another saucepan of water to the boil. Carefully place in the quails' eggs and boil for exactly one minute, and no more. Plunge into cold water and peel while still hot. Arrange the warm, dressed asparagus on the salad leaves. Quickly cut the quails' eggs in half and pop on top of the toast. They should still have runny yolks. Garnish with the black olives and serve immediately. Serves 4.

King Cob Soup

Sweetcorn is grown on the Island and distributed to the mainland under the name of King Cob. This simple soup epitomises the taste of late summer.

4 corn on the cob or two tins of sweetcorn
1 large onion, finely sliced
1 pt (570 ml) chicken or vegetable stock
1 level teaspoon of ground mace
generous pinch of cayenne pepper
¼ pt (150 ml) single cream

Strip the corn nibblets from the cobs with a sturdy knife. (Hold the knife at the top of the corn between the cob and the base of the nibblets. Push the knife down in one clean sweep. Do this all round the cob until the corn is removed). Discard the cobs. Put all the ingredients except the cream into a saucepan and simmer until the vegetables are soft. Purée in the blender. Return to the saucepan, add the cream, bring to the boil and serve. Serves 4.

The Town Hall, Newtown

Wild Chestnut Soup

If you are a keen walker, and the Island is the perfect place for such a pastoral activity, then the chances are you will eventually come upon an edible chestnut tree. The nuts can be recognised by their unfriendly, spikey, outer shell. Alternatively fresh chestnuts can be bought throughout the Island in the weeks prior to Christmas, and vacuum-packed chestnuts, obviously not as good as fresh, are available all year.

2 lb (900 gm) fresh chestnuts
1 carrot, 1 onion, oil
2 pt (1.1 lt) chicken or vegetable stock
½ tspn ground mace
½ tspn ground nutmeg
¼ tspn cayenne pepper
2 sugar lumps
salt and lots of black pepper

Slit the chestnut shells and put into a pan of boiling water and boil for 20 minutes. Cool slightly and remove the shells, protecting your hands with rubber gloves. Slice the onion, dice the carrot and soften both in a saucepan with a drop of oil. Add the peeled chestnuts and cook for 10 minutes more. Add the stock and the spices and simmer until the vegetables and chestnuts are soft and pulpy. Blend in the processor until smooth. Reheat. Serve with spicy croutons and a dollop of whipped cream. Serves 4.

Cucumber Pâté

The taste of cucumber is so refreshing summer wouldn't be the same without it. They are greenhouse grown on the Island for the mass market, but it is possible to find quantities of locally produced cucumbers at many of the small farm and village shops scattered throughout the Island.

2 large, crisp cucumbers
1 tbsp salt
1 oz (25 gm) finely chopped mint or dill weed
4 oz (110 gm) butter, softened to almost an oily state
1 tub Greek strained yoghurt or other plain yoghurt
5 fl oz tub double cream
1 sachet of gelatine crystals
lots of freshly ground black pepper

Line the bottom of a 1 pt (570 ml) terrine with greaseproof paper. Peel the cucumbers and grate. Put the grated flesh in a colander. Sprinkle with the salt and stand for 30 minutes until most of the liquid has drained away. Briefly rinse under the cold tap, squeeze dry and season liberally with the black pepper.

Soften the gelatine in 2 tbsp of cold water then dissolve the crystals over a pan of simmering water. Whisk the cream to the floppy stage.

Working quickly, beat the yoghurt into the oily butter, fold in the cucumber and chopped herbs, then the dissolved gelatine. Finally fold in the cream. Turn the mixture into the terrine and refrigerate for at least four hours, preferably overnight, until set.

Serve in neat slices with wholemeal toast and a few prawns to garnish. Serves 4 – 6.

Layered Crab Mousse

It is commonly acknowledged by the Islanders that crab has a better flavour than lobster. You will discover that local crab sandwiches are a popular lunchtime snack wherever you go; whether in a pub or one of numerous tearooms. This recipe is enhanced if served with a lightly flavoured curry mayonnaise.

8 oz (225 gm) brown crab meat
8 oz (225 gm) white crab meat
4 tbsp mayonnaise
small tub double cream
1 tbsp tomato ketchup
2 tbsp lemon juice
several dashes Tabasco sauce according to taste
1 lb (450 gm) large spinach leaves
salt and freshly ground black pepper
1 sachet of gelatine crystals

Put the brown and white crab meat in separate bowls. To the brown crab meat add 2 tbsp of mayonnaise and the tomato ketchup, and mix thoroughly. To the white crab meat add the remaining 2 tbsp of mayonnaise and the Tabasco sauce and mix thoroughly. Season both meats with salt and black pepper.

Blanch the spinach leaves in boiling water just long enough to wilt them. Then plunge into cold water to arrest the process. Line a 1 pt (570 ml) terrine dish with the spinach leaves, with enough hanging over the sides to fold back over the top.

Soften the gelatine crystals in the lemon juice with an extra tbsp of cold water, then heat gently in a double saucepan to melt the crystals.

Whip the cream until it is fairly stiff.

Working quickly mix half of the melted gelatine into the

brown crab mixture then fold in half the whipped cream. Pour into the bottom of the mould. Pop in the freezer for ten minutes to firm up quickly.

Mix the remaining melted gelatine with the white crab meat and fold in the rest of the whipped cream. Take the terrine out of the freezer and very carefully layer the white crab meat on top of the brown. Fold over the spinach leaves and put to chill in the refrigerator for four hours or overnight.

To serve, turn out of the terrine and cut into wedges. Pour a little curry mayonnaise around the edge and serve with toasted pitta bread. Serves 4 – 6.

Cheese, Garlic and Herb Pâté

One year, at the Garlic Festival, I served this pâté inside sticks of crisp celery. It was a tremendous success.

one 8 oz (225 gm) tub of cottage cheese
1 small tub of cream cheese
3-4 cloves of garlic
4 tbsp fresh, chopped, mixed herbs
4 spring onions, chopped including the green part
salt and lots of freshly ground black pepper

Place all the ingredients in a blender or liquidiser and process until smooth. Chill before serving to firm-up the pâté. Serve with toast, celery or apple slices. Serves 4 – 6.

Bembridge prawns are unique to the Isle of Wight. They are of a delicate size, with deep coral pink markings, but unfortunately they only enjoy a short season and sadly, some years we don't see them at all.

Bembridge Prawns with Coronation Dip

The Coronation Dip is a simplified version of the highly sophisticated sauce that was created in honour of the Coronation of Queen Elizabeth II in 1953. It makes a perfect accompaniment to these tiny crustaceans.

1 lb (450 gm) Bembridge prawns in their shell
juice of one lemon
Tabasco sauce according to taste
2 tbsp mayonnaise
1 small carton soured cream
1 chopped beef tomato
1 small, finely diced red pepper
1 chopped shallot, 2 tbsp oil
1 tbsp sweet mango pickle
1 tbsp mild curry paste

Toss the prawns in the lemon juice and Tabasco and refrigerate until ready to serve.

Heat the oil in the pan and gently cook the shallot, red pepper and tomato until they are soft and pulpy. Add the mango pickle and curry paste. Gently cook together for 5-6 minutes. Add the soured cream. Stir thoroughly for 1 minute. Put this sauce in a processor or liquidiser and blend until smooth. Pass through a sieve, then when cool stir in the mayonnaise. Chill before serving with the prawns, which can be arranged on a bed of crisp lettuce. Serves 4.

Wood Pigeon with Pickled Plum Sauce

I love to serve this dish in early autumn when both wood-pigeons and plums are in abundance on the Island.

4 wood pigeons' breasts
selection of bitter salad leaves i.e. radichio, curly endive
4 spring onions, shredded including the green part
1 mouli, grated and mixed with 1 tbsp salad dressing
1 tbsp corn oil and 1 tbsp sesame oil
8 oz (225 gm) fresh red plums
3 oz (75 gm) molasses sugar
1 chilli pepper, deseeded and finely sliced
1 or 2 cloves of garlic depending on personal taste
2 shallots, finely sliced
¼ pt (150 ml) vinegar
salt and black pepper

First make the sauce. Halve the plums and remove the stones. Put in a saucepan (preferably enamel or stainless steel) with the chilli pepper, the garlic that has been crushed with a scant tspn of salt, the shallot, vinegar, sugar and seasoning. Bring to the boil then lower the heat and simmer for 30 minutes. Cool the sauce until ready to serve.

  Season the pigeon breasts. Heat the corn and sesame oil in a frying pan and saute the pigeon 2-3 minutes each side. They should be cooked pink. (Over cooked pigeon tends to become tough). Meanwhile arrange the salad leaves and spring onions on plates. Put a spoonful of the plum sauce on the side, then arrange the warm pigeon breasts on top of the leaves. Serves 4.

It seems that the Romans, during their occupation of the Island, were particularly partial to oysters. Archaeological digs have uncovered a vast quantity of oyster shells in the vicinity of Roman villas.

In 1845 the Corporation of Newport owned seventy nine acres of oyster beds which were leased out to local fishermen. Unfortunately, over the years the oysters became diseased due to the increased amount of sewage that was released into the River Medina, and by 1870 Island fishmongers were refusing to sell them. Such problems are a thing of the past. Once again, Isle of Wight oysters are being harvested from the beds in Newtown Creek, and are extremely popular.

Newtown Oyster Stew

½ dozen oysters per person
2 shallots, finely chopped
1 oz (25 gm) butter, 1 tbsp oil
1 clove of garlic, crushed in 1 tspn of salt
small sachet of saffron powder
10 fl oz carton of soured cream
1 tbsp lemon juice
2 or 3 dashes of Tabasco sauce
¼ pt (150 ml) white wine
1 tbsp freshly chopped tarragon
1 carrot, cut into fine matchsticks
2 inch piece of cucumber, cut into fine matchsticks

Carefully open the oysters over a bowl to capture all the escaping juices. Put to one side.

Soften the shallot in the oil and butter. Do not allow to brown. Add the white wine, lemon juice, Tabasco, saffron, tarragon, crushed garlic, and the oyster juice. Simmer for about 5 minutes to suffuse the flavours. Add the cream and the carrot and cucumber. Simmer for about 10 minutes until a thin sauce forms.

Two minutes before serving add the oysters. They require only the briefest cooking.

Serve in soup plates, garnished with fresh herbs and a half oyster shell filled with extra soured cream seasoned with salt, black and cayenne pepper and a few grains of lumpfish roe.

Smoked Mackerel and Black Peppercorn Pâté

I obtain my smoked mackerel from Phillips at Binstead, who to my mind produce some of the best oak-smoked salmon, as well as mackerel, in the country. They also oak-smoke mussels, haddock, bloaters, kippers and chickens. This recipe has a lovely refreshing clean taste and is easy to make.

2 large smoked mackerel fillets
1 tbsp coarsely crushed black peppercorns
1 tbsp lemon juice
4 chopped spring onions
8 oz (225 gm) tub of cottage cheese
4 tbsp freshly chopped parsley

Remove the skin from the smoked mackerel fillets and put in a food blender with the rest of the ingredients. Whiz until smooth then chill in the refrigerator for 2-3 hours. Serve on a bed of crisp lettuce leaves with warm toast or pitta breads. Serves 4.

Baked Egg and Smoked Haddock en Cocotte

Duck eggs are nearly always available on the Island and because they have such a rich 'old fashioned' sort of yolk I tend to use them in this sort of dish, although hen eggs will do just as well.

4 free range eggs
1 small onion, finely chopped
2 tbsp oil
6 oz (175 gm) naturally smoked haddock
4 oz (110 gm) mature Cheddar cheese
10 fl oz pot of double cream
seasoning

Preheat the oven to its highest setting. It is essential that the eggs are put into an already hot oven.

Soften the onion in the oil - do not allow to brown. Divide the softened onion between four ramekin/cocotte dishes. Cut the smoked haddock into small cubes and arrange around the edge of the dishes. Break the eggs and put one in the centre of each dish. Grate the cheese and sprinkle over the eggs then pour the double cream equally over the dishes. Season with lots of black pepper and a sprinkling of salt.

Place on a baking sheet and bake in the very hot oven for 10 minutes, or longer if you prefer a well-done egg. N.B. Oven temperatures vary and you may have to try this dish a couple of times to get the eggs to the right 'set'. Serves 4.

Venison Gateau with Winter Sauce

1 lb (450 gm) cold, cooked venison
1 large onion, 2 thin slices of bread
1 egg, 1 dessertspoon curry paste
salt and pepper, 1 packet of vine leaves

Sauce
¼ pt (150 ml) port, ¼ pt (150 ml) orange juice
¼ pt (150 ml) game stock, 1 level tbsp honey
1 tbsp vinegar, 2 tbsp fresh cranberries
2 oz (50 gm) broken walnut pieces
salt and pepper, 1 level tbsp corn flour
2 oz (50 gm) butter (optional)

Mince or blend together the venison, onion, bread, curry paste and egg to a coarse mixture. Grease a 1 pt (570 ml) pudding basin and line with the vine leaves. (Individual gateaux can be made if preferred). Fill the basin with the venison mixture, lightly press down and cover with greaseproof paper or tin foil. Put in a roasting pan half filled with water and bake in the oven for 45 minutes. Gas 6/400f/200c.

To make the sauce put the port, stock, honey, vinegar, orange juice, walnuts, salt and pepper in a saucepan and simmer for 15 minutes to reduce slightly. Mix the cornflour with some water or more orange juice and stir into the sauce. Stirring continuously simmer until the sauce thickens. Adjust the seasoning. Cranberries tend to burst open then collapse when over-cooked so don't add them to the sauce until 8-10 minutes before serving. Add the butter to the sauce if using.

Turn the venison gateau onto a plate, pour the sauce over the top and serve in wedges with red cabbage salad. Serves 4.

FISH AND SHELLFISH

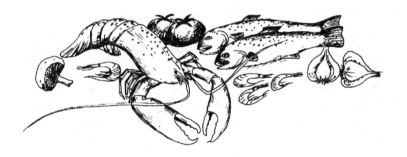

Chale Bay Mackerel with Lady Lowe's Mustard Sauce

1 large fresh mackerel per person
2 tbsp seasoned flour
oil for frying
¼ pt (150 ml) milk
¼ pt (150 ml) dry white wine
1 generous tbsp Isle of Wight coarse grain mustard

Clean out and fillet the mackerel. Ask your fishmonger to do this for you if you have problems with filleting fish. Leave the skins intact. Coat with the seasoned flour then shallow fry in a frying pan in the hot oil about 4 minutes each side. I like my mackerel to be crispy on the outside. Remove from the pan and keep warm.

To the same pan add a drop more oil, enough to make a roux with the remaining seasoned flour. Fry the flour in the oil for a couple of minutes without browning. Now add the milk and white wine. Blend together with a hand whisk until the sauce thickens.

One minute before serving stir in the mustard. It is essential that this is done at the last minute because the flavour of the mustard is often lost when overheated.

Wight Seafood Stew with Samphire

Also known as glasswort, samphire grows in brackish water, and can be collected during July and August in the many little estuaries found all over the Island.

There is a certain knack to eating it. Firstly, like asparagus it should be eaten with the hands. Bite on the thin hard thread that runs through its centre and pull the flesh off with your teeth. And as with asparagus, lashings of butter are essential.

A selection of locally caught fish to make
up 1.25 lb (550 gm) of meat.
For example: 1 large lobster, shelled
8 oz (225 gm) Bembridge prawns, shelled
12 oz (350 gm) piece of sea bass, unskinned and
cut into 1 inch cubes
4 small plaice fillets, rolled up and
secured with a cocktail stick
2 oz (50 gm) crab meat, 1 cuttlefish cut into rings
(other kinds of fish can be used but they should all
be cut, more or less into bite sized pieces)
1 onion, finely chopped
1 oz (25 gm) butter and 1 tbsp oil
the juice and finely grated rind of 1 orange
the juice and finely grated rind of 1 lemon
½ pt (275 ml) dry white wine
1 tbsp freshly chopped parsley
1 tbsp freshly chopped dill weed
1 tbsp freshly chopped sorrel leaves
piece of lemon grass, finely chopped without
the woody bit, salt and pepper
¼ tspn ground coriander seeds
½ pt (275 ml) single cream
½ pt (275 ml) fish stock made with the lobster shell,

prawn shells and any trimmings from the fish. N.B. Fish
stock should never be cooked for more than 30 minutes;
after this its flavour can become bitter
12 oz (350 gm) samphire

Soften the onion in the butter in a pan large enough to eventually take all the listed ingredients.

Add the lemon juice and rind, the orange juice and rind, white wine, lemon grass, coriander and fish stock. Simmer rapidly for 15-20 minutes until reduced by half.

Add the cream and simmer for a further 10 minutes. At this stage the recipe can be put on hold until five minutes before you want to serve it.

To the simmering sauce add the herbs then the fish in this order: first the firm fish such as sea bass, salmon, cod, haddock, second the more delicate fish such as sole and plaice unless it is rolled up then add this first, next cuttlefish rings which only require a minutes cooking and finally anything that has been pre-cooked, such as lobster and prawns that need nothing more than reheating.

Prepare the samphire by washing well in lots of clean running water. Trim off any woody ends. Bring a large pan of salted water to the boil then plunge in the samphire and simmer rapidly for about 8 minutes until tender. Drain. Toss in butter or olive oil.

Arrange the samphire in the centre of soup plates and surround with the delicious fish stew.

For a less fattening dish replace the cream with skimmed milk mixed into 2 tspn of cornflour and add at the same time as the stock and fruit juice etc. Serves 4.

Aromatic Lobster

The lobster fishing industry is important to the Island. From a customer's point of view they are also substantially cheaper than on the mainland, so I strongly advise that you keep a watchful eye on their price at the Island's fishmongers – especially during July and August.

4 live lobsters
8 oz (225 gm) butter
½ pt (275 ml) white wine
¼ tspn ground mace
¼ tspn freshly ground black pepper
4 tbsp freshly chopped mixed tender herbs i.e. sorrel, dill,
tarragon, coriander, mint and parsley, at least four types
4 thin slices fresh lemon

Boil the lobsters for 8 minutes in plenty of water. Cool. Remove the shell by splitting in half length ways. Keep one half of each shell to serve as a container for the finished dish.

Melt the butter in a large pan. Add the wine, lemon and spices. Simmer for 4-5 minutes to form a rich sauce. Now add the herbs and seasoning and heat for 1 minute. Add the lobster meat, heat through for a further 2 or 3 minutes. Do not allow to boil or over-heat. If the sauce becomes oily add a drop more wine or water to emulsify. Serve this delicious ambrosia in lobster shells with home-made pasta ribbons. Serves 4.

Lobster Risotto

one 2 lb (900 gm) live lobster
¼ pt (150 ml) white wine
8 oz (225 gm) arborio or pudding rice
2 crushed cloves garlic
2 finely chopped shallots
2 oz (50 gm) butter
grated rind and juice of 1 lemon
2 tbsp chopped parsley
2 tbsp double cream
salt and black pepper

Cook the lobster in 2 pt (1.1 lt) vegetable stock for 12 minutes. Cool. Remove meat from shell and coarsely chop.

Simmer the lobster shells in the cooking water for half an hour. Strain and keep the stock hot by the side of the risotto pan. (A large heavy bottomed saucepan or frying pan will do). Soften the onion and garlic in the butter. Do not brown. Then add the rice and stir round until it becomes transparent. Add the wine and stir until absorbed. Gradually add the simmering lobster stock until it is all absorbed and the rice is cooked. This will take 20-30 minutes. Please note that risotto should be wet. Season. Add the lemon juice, the finely grated lemon peel and the cream. Heat through. Then add the lobster meat, and reheat through for 2-3 minutes. Serves 4.

Lobster and Salmon Pie with Red Pepper Sauce

Most recipes call for lobster to be reheated. It is therefore essential that you don't over-cook it in the first place. If I am making lobster ravioli or a pie, I cook a 1 lb lobster for a mere five minutes, just long enough to firm up the flesh, and make it easy to handle.

two 1 lb (450 gm) lobsters
8 oz (225 gm) of fresh salmon – the tail piece will do for
this recipe if its cheaper
1 tbsp fresh chopped dill weed or mint
¼ pt (150 ml) double cream
1 red pepper, thinly sliced then cut into 1 inch lengths
lots of black pepper and a generous pinch of salt
8 oz (225 gm) shortcrust pastry

Soften the red pepper in a little oil until soft then cool. Cook the lobsters in lots of boiling water for 5 minutes. Remove the lobster meat from their shells and cut into large dice. Remove the skin from the salmon and purée in the blender. Remove the salmon from the blender and add the dill weed or mint and the cream. Mix to a smooth paste then add the diced lobster and the red pepper.

Divide the pastry in half and roll out each half to fit into a 7 inch flan ring. Turn the salmon and lobster mixture into the pastry-lined flan ring and cover with the rest of the pastry rolled out as thinly as possible.

Bake in a preheated oven gas 7/425f/220c for 30 minutes. Serve hot or cold with a crisp salad and red pepper sauce. Serves 4.

Red Pepper Sauce
1 large diced red pepper
1 small clove of garlic

1 small onion, diced
2 ripe tomatoes, quartered
2 tbsp olive oil
1 small carton of soured cream
salt and pepper and Tabasco

Soften the red pepper, garlic, onion and tomato very slowly in the oil until a thick pulp is formed. Press through a sieve and when cold stir into the soured cream. Season with the salt, pepper and Tabasco, and serve chilled.

CHALE BAY MACKEREL

Before the last World War mackerel was a major source of fresh fish for the Islanders. At the beginning of every summer a lookout was posted on the clifftop at Chale Bay to watch for the first sign of the vast shoals that annually entered the Bay. As soon as the lookout alerted the fishermen they put to sea, dragging large seine nets behind their boats. The nets were rowed round the mackerel in a large sweep, until the fish were contained within the arc. The nets were then drawn in until the mackerel, in their thousands, could be scooped into baskets from the shore line. As far back as 1796, Sprake, the Isle of Wight carriers, were delivering freshly caught mackerel around the Island.

The beginning of this prolific mackerel season was celebrated every year with the 'Mackerel Fair', which is still held to this day, though it is more of a commiseration than a celebration as the shoals disappeared after the 1930's. The fair is held on the third week in June. Fresh mackerel, smoked mackerel and mackerel pâté are sold from stalls. The Niton Hash House Harriers mount a mackerel run to commemorate the race to get the first basket of fish to the village.

Char Grilled Mackerel with
Fresh Tomato Chutney

The essence of this dish is that the mackerel should be crisply cooked so that the flavour of the skin is enhanced. Mackerel should only be bought if freshly caught and a sparkling steel blue colour. After that the flavour rapidly deteriorates.

4 large or 8 small mackerel, heads removed and cleaned
a flavoured oil for basting i.e. chilli oil
2 beefsteak tomatoes
1 tbsp each of freshly chopped parsley, mint and coriander
4 spring onions
1 green pepper
3 tbsp olive oil
juice of one lime or lemon

First get the barbecue ready. Brush the mackerel and the wire grill with oil. When the coals are white hot arrange the mackerel on top of the oiled rack. Cook on one side until crispy and slightly charred (about 10 minutes) turn onto the other side and char grill for a further 10 minutes. To obtain a really crispy, dry flesh and skin it is best to take as long as possible over a not too hot grill so that the fish cooks crispy without burning.

To make the relish. Remove the pips from the tomatoes and chop into small dice (some of you may prefer to remove the tomato skins, but this takes away the fibre element).

Put the green pepper, spring onion, herbs, oil and lime juice in a food processor. Blend until smooth. Stir into the chopped tomatoes. Season with salt and pepper. Serve the relish with the mackerel, a crisp green salad and crusty bread. Serves 4.

Marinated Mackerel

Served cold, this is a delightful summer luncheon dish. I like it with fresh malted granary bread and tomato and olive salad.

4 mackerel, cleaned and filleted but leave the skins intact
2 roughly chopped beef tomatoes
½ each red, yellow and green pepper, finely sliced
1 small finely sliced onion
1 small finely sliced bulb of fennel
juice and rind of 1 lemon or lime
2 tbsp white wine vinegar
2 tbsp fresh chopped parsley
2 tbsp fresh chopped coriander leaves
4 tbsp olive oil
2 oz (50 gm) plain flour seasoned with ½ tspn salt, ½ tspn ground black pepper and 1 tspn Chinese five spice powder

Toss the mackerel fillets in the seasoned flour and shallow fry 4 minutes each side in the olive oil. Arrange in a shallow dish that will take all of the mackerel without them over-lapping. Put to one side.

Soften the onions, fennel and peppers in more olive oil. Add the tomatoes and cook until soft. Add the lemon rind, juice, vinegar and herbs. Stir around and cook briefly for 1-2 minutes.

Pour over the mackerel fillets, cover and cool. When cold put in the fridge to chill. Serve with salad. Serves 4.

Sea bass is one of England's greatest glories, with a price to match. But if nothing else it is plentiful around the Isle of Wight and its freshness is guaranteed.

Bass has a delicious, moist, firm, meaty flesh and a pretty delicate silvery skin that I always leave intact. Having become – because of the price – such a special occasion fish the next three recipes are intended to reflect that fact.

Sea Bass with Saffron and Scallops

2 sea bass – each about 1 lb (450 gm) in weight
8 fresh scallops, ½ pt (275 ml) dry white wine
½ pt (275 ml) fish stock made from the bones
1 small sachet of saffron strands or powder
1 large onion, 1 clove of garlic
4 tbsp double cream or 4 tbsp milk mixed with
2 tspn cornflour, salt and pepper

Remove the large scales and the head from the fish and then fillet. Be careful how you do this as sea bass bones are very spikey and can give you a nasty stab. (If in doubt ask your fishmonger to do it for you but make sure he gives you the bones and head for the stock).

Lay the fish in a shallow roasting pan surrounded with a scant ½ inch of water or white wine. Cover with tin foil to seal in the steam and bake in a hot oven preheated to gas 7/425f/220c for 20 minutes. Be careful not to over-cook the fish. Test at the 15 minutes stage with a skewer. If it slides through the fish easily then it is done.

Meanwhile make the sauce. You may want to start this before you put the fish in to cook. In a saucepan put the white wine, fish stock, saffron, garlic and the onion which has been skinned and cut into quarters. Simmer gently until the stock has reduced by half and the onion is soft and pulpy. Add the cream or the cornflour blended with the milk and in the latter case, stirring all the time, simmer for a further 15 minutes. When thickened put in a blender, whiz until smooth and then pass through a sieve. Return to the saucepan. Season to taste (at this stage the sea bass can be put in the oven to cook).

Roughly chop the scallops and five minutes before serving the dish pop the scallops into the simmering sauce. This is just long enough to cook them without over-cooking. Arrange the sea bass fillets on individual plates and surround with the delicious sauce. Serves 4.

Sea Bass with Garden Sorrel Sauce and Cucumber Spaghetti

2 sea bass each about 1 lb (450 gm) in weight
2 oz (50 gm) fresh sorrel leaves
½ pt (275 ml) white wine
½ pt (275 ml) fish stock made from the
fish bones and head, 1 large onion
1 clove of garlic, 2 oz (50 gm) butter
4 tbsp double cream or 4 tbsp milk mixed with
2 tspn cornflour, salt and pepper
1 large firm cucumber
1 tbsp freshly chopped tarragon

Remove the large scales and the head from the fish and then fillet. Be careful how you do this as sea bass bones are very spikey and can give you a nasty stab. (If in doubt ask your fishmonger to do it for you but make sure he gives you the bones and head for the stock).

Lay the fish in a shallow roasting pan surrounded with a scant ½ inch of water or white wine. Cover with tin foil to seal in the steam and bake in a hot oven, preheated to gas 7/425f/220c for 20 minutes. Be careful not to over cook the fish. Test at the 15 minutes stage with a skewer. If it slides through the fish easily then it is done.

To prepare the cucumber spaghetti. Peel away the skin of the cucumber. Cut in half horizontally then each of these halves in half vertically. Remove the seeds in the centre and discard. Now cut the cucumber into long thin spaghetti sized strips. Place in a colander, sprinkle with the salt and stand for 30 minutes.

Meanwhile make the sauce. You may want to start this before you cook the fish. In a saucepan put the wine, fish stock, garlic, washed sorrel leaves that have been ripped up into smaller pieces and the onion that has been skinned and quartered. Simmer until the liquid has reduced by slightly more than half. Add the cream or milk and cornflour, and in the latter case, stirring all the time, simmer for a further 15 minutes. Put the sauce in a blender, whiz until smooth and return to the saucepan to keep warm while the fish is cooking. Add half the butter to the sauce to enrich it.

Five minutes before ready to serve, rinse the cucumber and plunge into a saucepan of boiling water. Boil rapidly for a scant five minutes or until the cucumber wilts. Drain and toss the remaining butter and chopped tarragon into the cucumber.

To serve, arrange the fish fillets on individual plates. Top with the cucumber spaghetti and surround with the sorrel sauce. Serves 4.

Sea Bass with Crab and Red Pepper Sauce

1 sea bass about 3 lb (1.4 kg) in weight
6 oz (175 gm) brown and white crab meat, mixed together
salt and pepper and a dash of Tabasco
1 pt (570 ml) fish stock made from the bones and head
½ pt (275 ml) dry white wine
1 large red pepper
1 large onion
1 clove of garlic
1 oz (25 gm) butter
2 tbsp double cream
salt and pepper
2 tbsp chopped chives
2 tbsp chopped chervil or fennel leaves
more salt and pepper

Remove the large scales and the head from the fish and then fillet. Be careful how you do this as sea bass bones are very spikey and can give you a nasty stab. (If in doubt ask your fishmonger to do it for you but make sure he gives you the bones and head for the stock).

Cut each fillet into three equal sized pieces. You should end up with four squarish shapes and two long tail piece shapes. (The tail ends will be narrow so don't forget to cut them a little longer than the square pieces of fish. To make the tail pieces square tuck the pointed end underneath).

Cut a slit into the side of the flesh of the fish steaks to form a little pocket. Season the crab meat with the salt, pepper and Tabasco and divide between the six pockets. Push the fish back together to seal in the crabmeat.

Arrange flesh-side down in a greased shallow roasting tin. Surround the fish with a scant amount of water or white wine. Seal with tin foil and bake in a preheated oven gas 7/425f/220c for 20 minutes. Be careful not to over cook the fish. Test at the 15 minute stage with a skewer. If it slides through the fish easily, then it is done.

Meanwhile make the sauce which can in fact be prepared in advance then reheated. In a saucepan put the stock, white wine, onion which has been skinned and coarsely sliced and the garlic. Simmer until reduced to ½ pt (275 ml) of liquid.

Finely dice the red pepper into small confetti sized pieces. Add this to the sauce with the cream, butter and herbs.

Simmer rapidly for 10 minutes, then serve with the crab stuffed sea bass. Serves 6.

Crab and Silver Beet Tart

6 oz (175 gm) short pastry, made with:
6 oz (175 gm) plain flour, 2 oz (50 gm) lard

2 oz (50 gm) butter, 2 tspn celery salt
6 oz (175 gm) brown and white crab meat
8 oz (225 gm) silver beet, 1 egg
¼ pt (150 ml) single cream
4 oz (110 gm) cream cheese

Line a 7 inch flan ring with the pastry. Chill in the fridge.

Wash the silver beet. Tear up the leaves and cut the stems into 1 inch pieces. Put in a saucepan with a knob of butter and cook on a low heat until the beet has wilted. Squeeze out any excess water and when cold put in the bottom of the flan ring.

Mix together the crab meat, cream cheese, egg and single cream. Pour over the silver beet then bake in a preheated oven gas 5/375f/190c for 45 minutes.

Delicious served hot or cold with salad. Serves 4.

Like mackerel, herrings are caught in large numbers around the Island's waters. Herrings enjoy a long season, from June to March, but I think they are at their best at the beginning of the season when they are small enough to serve two per person.

In the 13th century the old equivalent of 10p could buy as many as 300 herrings. They were a good and nutritious meal for the ploughmen harvesting at the time of this seasonal glut.

Traditionally they were served soused in vinegar or boiled in brine in an attempt to preserve them, and, like most cooks, I am delighted the invention of the refrigerator makes this practise no longer a necessity. Nevertheless the tradition of soused herrings has stayed with us, and I have devised a slightly more delicate pickled herring dish.

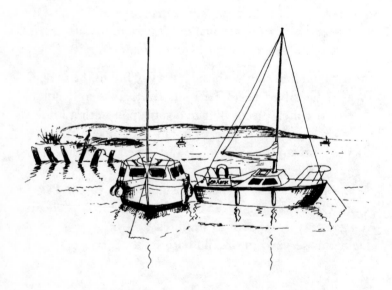

Aromatic Pickled Herrings (or Mackerel)

4 large or 8 small very fresh herrings (or mackerel)
1 pt (570 ml) white wine vinegar
the juice and grated rind of 1 lemon
the juice and grated rind of 1 lime
1 tbsp pickling spice
1 tbsp fennel seeds
1 blade of lemon grass, cut into 1 inch lengths
1 tspn of salt
2 oz (50 gm) castor sugar
2 bay leaves
1 fresh chilli, seeds removed then shredded
2 large onions, finely sliced

Thoroughly clean and fillet the herrings. Arrange in a shallow dish that will take all the fillets without them overlapping. Put in the fridge until ready to use.

Put all the remaining ingredients in a saucepan and bring to the boil. Lower the heat and simmer gently for 30 minutes.

Remove the herrings from the fridge and pour the hot pickling liquid over the fish. Cover with cling film or tin foil and put to one side until the liquid is completely cold. Refrigerate until ready to serve. This dish will keep for several days.

Delicious served with terrine of baby leeks (see chapter on salads and vegetables) and a mustard dressing. Serves 4.

Herrings in Oatmeal with Gooseberry Sauce

4 large fresh herrings
4 tbsp medium oatmeal
salt and pepper
olive oil for frying
8 oz (225 gm) gooseberries
4 oz (110 gm) castor sugar
(use less sugar for a sharper taste)
1 oz (25 gm) fresh chopped mint
2 oz (50 gm) butter

Thoroughly clean then fillet the herrings. Season with salt and pepper then coat in the oatmeal, pressing the oats to the damp flesh. Put to one side while you make the sauce.

Top and tail the gooseberries and put in an enamel or stainless steel saucepan with the chopped mint, castor sugar and the butter. Cover with a lid and stew very gently over a low heat for 30 minutes until a sauce has formed. Keep warm.

Heat the oil in a large frying pan and when hot sâuté the herring fillets about 4 minutes each side or until the oat-meal turns a delicious crunchy golden brown. Serve immediately with the warm gooseberry sauce and a crisp green side salad.

N.B. Traditionally this sauce is served with mackerel so keep an open mind when shopping and buy whichever fish is freshest. Serves 4.

I don't know why this should be, but local Isle of Wight plaice always seems to be plumper than other plaice. It is available all year round but is at its best in late summer.

Fillets of Plaice with Bembridge Prawns and Bacon

2 or 3 fillets of plaice per person
seasoned flour
6 oz (175 gm) Bembridge prawns, shells removed
4 oz (110 gm) smoked streaky bacon, diced
2 oz (50 gm) butter
1 tbsp oil
juice of half a lemon
¼ pt (150 ml) white wine
2 tbsp freshly chopped parsley
salt and pepper

Toss the plaice fillets in the seasoned flour. Gently heat the oil and butter in a heavy-bottomed frying pan. Add the diced bacon and cook for about 5 minutes until turning crisp. (It is essential this is done slowly so that the butter doesn't burn).

Push the bacon to the side of the pan and add the plaice fillets. Cook 3 minutes each side. Add the white wine, lemon juice, parsley and prawns to the pan. Raise the heat slightly and shaking the pan around to mix in the ingredients. Cook for a further 2 minutes.

Serve with new potatoes and mange tout. Serves 4.

Fillets of Plaice Florentine

3 large or 4 small plaice fillets per person
2 lb (900 gm) spinach leaves
2 oz (50 gm) butter
1 oz (25 gm) butter
1 oz (25 gm) flour
¾ pt (450 ml) milk
6 oz (175 gm) grated mature Cheddar cheese
salt and pepper

Remove the skins from the plaice fillets and roll up into cylinders.

Wash the spinach and tear into smaller pieces. Squash into a saucepan, add 2 oz (50 gm) of butter, season with salt and pepper and tightly seal with a lid. Cook very gently over a low heat until the spinach has completely wilted. Remove the lid, raise the heat slightly and cook for a further 15 minutes or until the water from the spinach has virtually evaporated. Arrange this spinach on the bottom of a baking dish. Arrange the cylinders of plaice on top of the spinach.

Make a cheese sauce with the rest of the ingredients. Melt the butter in a saucepan. Toss in the flour and cook on a low heat for about 5 minutes. Whisking all the time, add the milk to this flour mix, then bring to the boil. Lower the heat and simmer until the sauce thickens. Season to taste. Add the grated cheese and stir thoroughly.

Pour the cheese sauce over the plaice cylinders. Pop into a hot preheated oven gas 7/425f/220c and bake for 30 minutes. The top should be a nice golden brown when done. Serve with new potatoes and French beans. Serves 4.

Plaice Olives with Mussels and Summer Tomato Sauce

3 or 4 fillets of plaice per person depending on the size
4 oz (110 gm) smoked mussels
2 oz (50 gm) cream cheese, butter
1 lb (450 gm) tomatoes, skinned (optional) and chopped
2 cloves of garlic, crushed in ½ tspn salt
lots of black pepper
2 tbsp olive oil
1 small finely chopped onion
1 tbsp tomato purée
2 tbsp freshly chopped oregano or marjoram
¼ pt (150 ml) white wine
1 tbsp black olives in oil, stoned and coarsely chopped

Remove the skin from the plaice fillets. Chop the smoked mussels and mix with the cream cheese. Spread this mixture on the plaice fillets then roll them up. Put the plaice rolls in a baking dish. Dot with plenty of butter, cover with tin foil and bake for 30 minutes in a hot oven gas 7/425f/220c.

Meanwhile make the sauce. Put the olive oil in a frying pan. Add the onion and garlic and sâuté slowly for 5 minutes to soften the onion. Add the rest of the ingredients. Stir well and simmer gently for 30 minutes until a sauce forms. If it gets too dry add a drop of water.

Serve the sauce with the plaice fillets and a crisp green salad. Serves 4.

Cod Steaks with Oyster Sauce

Gone are the days when cod was considered poor man's food. It now seems quite fitting to honour this undeniably good tasting, chunky fleshed fish with a creamy oyster sauce.

4 cod steaks
seasoned flour
oil for frying
¼ pt (150 ml) fish stock or preferably juice from the oysters
8 oysters, roughly chopped
¼ pt (150 ml) white wine
several dashes of Tabasco sauce or a generous pinch cayenne pepper
1 tbsp lemon juice
1 tbsp chopped dill weed or fennel leaves
5 fl oz carton double cream

Toss the cod steaks in the seasoned flour and fry in the oil for 5 minutes each side. Remove from the pan and keep warm. The fish will still continue to cook slightly.

To the same pan add the fish stock, white wine, lemon juice, Tabasco, and dill weed. Simmer for 10 minutes to amalgamate the flavours and reduce the liquid. Add the double cream. Raise the heat and simmer until a thick sauce forms.

Three minutes before serving add the chopped oysters. It is essential that the oysters are not over-cooked as they lose their lovely creamy texture. Arrange a cod steak on each plate and pour over the sauce. Garnish with a slice of lemon, a twirl of whipped cream and a sprig of dill weed. Serves 4.

SALADS AND VEGETABLES

GARLIC

The production of garlic on the Isle of Wight has become a major marketing success story, although ironically most of the crop is sold to the French market. Every August the garlic harvest is celebrated with the Garlic Festival held at Arreton; where you will find weird and wonderful things done with the pungent bulbs that leave you in no doubt garlic is on the menu.

For the true convert, garlic isn't used delicately – a clove at a time to lightly enhance the flavour of a dish – but by the bulb to exaggerate the garlic flavour. A must for gourmets is the 'green' newly harvested bulb, which can be bought fresh early in summer. Sweet, hot and juicy, it makes a wonderful relish when mixed with fresh parsley, capers and olive oil.

In the past garlic has been a mere seasoning. Because of its complex scientific make-up it has a stronger flavour when crushed than when it is left whole. Indeed left whole, and cooked for a long period, its taste becomes extremely mild. As a seasoning, use half a clove wiped around the surface of a salad bowl to impart a sober flavour, crush just one clove to go in a sauce, or pop in a whole unbruised clove to lightly flavour mayonnaise.

Best of all use garlic for the sake of garlic. Make it the focal point of a dish. Serve garlic soup, garlic mousseline, garlic purée or sauce, and why not serve it as a vegetable? Not such a wild idea once you have tried it.

Roast Garlic

Delicious with barbecued steak or lamb.

1 whole bulb of garlic per person, butter
drop of chicken or vegetable stock

Keep the bulb intact but at the same time remove the outer skins. The skins that cover the individual cloves can the left on. Arrange the whole bulbs snugly in a well buttered, shallow baking dish. Season and dot with more butter. Bake for approx 1 hour gas 4/180c/350f. Halfway through cooking baste with a little vegetable or chicken stock.

Smoked Garlic Timbales

Smoked garlic has a rather delicate flavour and this recipe will go as well with fish, such as bass, turbot and monkfish as it will with any kind of meat.

2 large bulbs of smoked garlic, 3 large eggs
2 large coarsely chopped onions
1 pt (570 ml) single cream, 2 tbsp chopped parsley

Break open the bulbs and skin the cloves. Put in a saucepan with the onion and single cream. Simmer gently until the onion and garlic are soft. Blend this mixture in a food processor until smooth. Add the eggs and parsley and blend again.

Heavily butter 4 generous ¼ pt (150 ml) moulds (ramekins or teacups are ideal). Pour the mixture into the moulds then set in a roasting pan half filled with water.

Cover with foil and put in a medium hot oven, gas 5/375f/190c for 30-40 minutes or until set and slightly risen.

To serve run a knife around the edges and turn out. Can be served as a starter with an Italian tomato sauce. Serves 4.

Pan-Fried Tomatoes with Herbs and Smoked Garlic

Terrific served with grilled meats or as a simple starter.

8 tomatoes
4 cloves of smoked garlic
2 oz (50 gm) butter
2 tbsp good olive oil, pinch of salt
masses of freshly ground black pepper
1 tbsp each of freshly chopped, basil, sorrel, marjoram,
dill, mint and parsley

Cut the tomatoes in half. Remove the papery skins from the garlic and finely chop. Melt the butter and oil in a frying pan large enough to take all the tomatoes. When the butter has melted add the tomatoes to the pan flat sides facing downwards and the chopped garlic. Add the pinch of salt and as much black pepper as you have patience to grind. Cook the tomatoes very slowly so that they don't singe and the garlic doesn't brown. After about 8 minutes turn the tomatoes over and add the chopped herbs and more black pepper. Cook gently for a further 8 minutes until the tomatoes are cooked and the herbs have wilted. Serve straight from the pan. Serves 4.

Terrine of Baby Leeks

Strictly speaking, leeks are a winter vegetable, so this terrine is best made at the beginning of the season when the leeks are still tiny (no more than ½ inch thick).

2 lb (900 gm) baby leeks
salt and lots of black pepper
1 small finely chopped clove of garlic
1 tbsp finely chopped fresh thyme or sage
Dressing: 4 tbsp olive oil, 1 tbsp white wine vinegar
1 tbsp tarragon mustard, pinch of sugar
1 tspn of lightly crushed white mustard seeds

Trim and clean the leeks, but leave as much of the green part as possible intact. Place the leeks in a colander over a pan of simmering water or steamer and steam until tender.

Mix together the garlic and chopped herb. Lightly oil a 1 pt (570 ml) terrine and arrange a layer of leeks on the bottom. Season with salt, pepper and some of the garlic and herbs. Continue these layers until all the leeks are used up. Make sure the layers are alternated in such a way that you have the green part of the leek at both ends of the terrine. The leeks should come up above the top of the terrine. Cover with cling film or foil then weight down to compress the leeks. Put in the fridge still weighed down and leave overnight to chill.

To serve, put the dressing ingredients in a jar and shake together. Carefully turn out the leek terrine and with a very sharp knife cut ½ inch thick slices. Still handling the terrine carefully lay one or two slices on a plate and pour some of the mustard dressing over the top. Serves 4.

Asparagus with Orange Butter Sauce

2 lb (900 gm) quality asparagus
1 large orange
¼ pt (150 ml) medium white wine, or light chicken stock
4 oz (110 gm) quality butter
1 tbsp double cream
seasoning

Cut off the woody base of the spears. With a potato peeler remove the fine outer skin (this is not compulsory). Fill a large pan that will take the asparagus lying flat on the bottom with water. Bring the water to the boil and carefully drop in the asparagus. Cook for 8-10 minutes depending on which grade you are using. Remove from the pan with a fish slice and drain flat on a wire rack.

Finely grate the rind from the orange and put in a heavy bottomed saucepan with the white wine and the juice of the orange. Bring to the boil. Simmer for 1 minute. Dice the butter. Lower the heat under the orange flavoured wine and gradually, a piece at a time, whisk in the butter. Don't let the liquid come to the boil otherwise the butter will become oily and separate. When all the butter is used up, whisk in the cream. This will act as a stabiliser. But don't take this too literally, you must still avoid boiling the sauce. Season and serve poured over the asparagus. Serves 4.

Asparagus and Cream Cheese Roulade

1 lb (450 gm) fresh spinach
½ oz (10 gm) butter
4 large eggs, separated
salt and lots of black pepper
pinch of nutmeg
1 tbsp grated Parmesan cheese
8 oz (225 gm) cream cheese
8 oz (225 gm) asparagus spears
1 tbsp freshly chopped chervil

Wash the spinach and remove the stalks. Put in a large pan with the butter, seal with a lid and cook slowly until thoroughly wilted. Put in a blender and whiz to a purée.

Line a large Swiss roll tin or a roasting tin with greaseproof paper and brush liberally with oil.

Whisk the egg yolks into the spinach purée and season with the salt, pepper and nutmeg. Whisk the egg whites until stiff but not dry and fold into the spinach. Start off with just a tablespoon of egg white to slacken the mixture off then carefully fold in the rest of the white.

Pour in to the Swiss roll tin and smooth out. Bake in a preheated oven for gas 7/425f/220c for 10-15 minutes until the top feels firm.

Sprinkle the Parmesan on a flat surface and turn the roulade out onto this then peel off the greaseproof paper backing while still warm. Trim the edges of the roulade.

To make the filling, trim the woody bits off the asparagus then cut into 1 inch lengths. Boil in plenty of water for 8 minutes then drain and refresh in cold water.

When the asparagus is cold mix with the cream cheese, salt and pepper and chervil. Spread this mixture over the roulade and roll up. To serve, cut into slices and arrange on a bed of curly endive. If wished, sprinkle with more grated Parmesan cheese. Serves 6.

During the autumn the Island is a rich source of wild mushrooms, and during the summer months Parasol mushrooms are easily found. But unless you are an expert on what you can and can't safely eat I strongly advise that you leave well alone.

Cultivated mushrooms are grown for local consumption in the disused railway tunnel at Whitwell.

Marinated Mushrooms

It is now possible to buy a wide variety of mushrooms in the shops. For this recipe you could use: mushrooms 'ordinaire', chestnut mushrooms, oyster mushrooms or shitake mushrooms or a mixture of them all.

a generous 1 lb (450 gm) mushrooms
1 small onion, finely chopped
2 cloves of garlic, crushed in a tspn of salt
juice of 1 lemon
4 tbsp olive oil
¼ pt (150 ml) red wine
black pepper
2 tbsp freshly chopped parsley

Wash and dry the mushrooms. Slice thickly then toss in the lemon juice. Heat the olive oil in a pan and gently fry the mushrooms and onions for 15 minutes. Add the crushed garlic, black pepper, red wine and parsley and cook gently for a further five minutes. Serve cold with cold meats and pâtés. Serves 4.

Broad Bean Purée with Fennel

Beans were a staple crop on the Island in the 1790's when arable farming was at its height. Even today the heavy chalk soil on parts of the Island seems to particularly suit broad beans.

Although at their best when picked young, this recipe is perfect for using up large overgrown beans.

2 lb (900 gm) broad beans
1 tbsp lemon juice
1 tbsp fennel seeds
salt and pepper
2 oz (50 gm) butter or 4 tbsp olive oil
2 tbsp cream

Shell the beans then cook them with the fennel seeds in a pan of boiling water for 15-20 minutes or until tender. Strain through a fine sieve in order to retain the fennel seeds. Put the beans in a blender with the lemon juice, salt and pepper, butter and cream. Whiz to a purée. Serve piping hot with fish, chicken or lamb. Serves 4.

Green Vegetable Medley

Serve in early summer when all the vegetables are small, young and tender. Any green vegetables can be used. For instance: asparagus cut into 2 inch lengths: tiny broccoli florets, mange tout, Kenya beans, French beans cut into 2 inch lengths, green peppers cut into 2 inch lengths and ¼ inch wide, courgettes cut into ¼ inch wide and 2 inch lengths.

A total of 1 lb (450 gm) of a mixture of any of the above
vegetables
4 tbsp good olive oil
juice of half a lemon
salt and black pepper
1 tbsp freshly chopped mixed herbs or just parsley
1 chopped, hard boiled egg
1 tbsp toasted, brown breadcrumbs

Cook the vegetables individually in boiling water until just cooked. Drain then mix together. Toss in the rest of the ingredients and serve immediately. Serves 4.

Living in the south in so mild a climate we are lucky enough to have new seasons carrots as early as April. The orange seems to have a natural affinity with carrots, as the following three recipes demonstrate.

Aromatic Carrot Salad

1 lb (450 gm) carrots, scraped or finely peeled
the finely grated rind and juice of 1 orange
2 oz (50 gm) finely grated cream of coconut
1 tbsp corn oil
1 tbsp sesame oil
1 tbsp toasted sesame seeds
1 tbsp dry roasted poppy seeds
1 tspn dry toasted caraway seeds
pinch of salt and pepper

Grate the carrot as finely as possible to match the size of the grated cream of coconut. Mix in a bowl with the coconut, sesame seeds, poppy seeds and caraway seeds. Mix together the orange juice and rind and the two oils. Stir into the carrot salad and stand for about 1 hour to amalgamate the flavours. Serves 4.

Carrots a la Grecque

1 lb (450 gm) carrots, scraped or finely peeled
1 red onion, finely sliced
1 tbsp currants
the juice and grated rind of 1 orange
¼ pt (150 ml) white wine
1 level tbsp castor sugar
1 oz (25 gm) butter
salt and pepper

Cut the carrots into slices or sticks. Put in a saucepan with the rest of the ingredients. Cover with a lid and simmer on a low heat for 20 minutes or until the carrots are tender. Take off the lid, raise the heat and simmer rapidly until the carrots are glistening and the liquid reduced to almost nothing. Serve with roast beef or venison. Serves 4.

Carrot and Orange Purée

Ideal for old, tough carrots.

1 lb (450 gm) carrots, scraped or thinly peeled
the finely grated rind of 1 orange
1 oz (25 gm) butter
salt and pepper

Slice the carrots and cook in a pan of boiling water until very tender. Put into a processor, or pass through a mouli mill, and blend with the orange rind and butter. Season to taste and serve with virtually anything including fish.

POULTRY, GAME AND
OTHER MEAT

Char-Grilled Chicken with Rosemary and Garlic Butter

4 boned chicken breasts, wings left intact
small bunch of fresh young rosemary
8 cloves of garlic
¼ pt (150 ml) olive oil
4 oz (110 gm) butter
pinch cayenne pepper according to taste

Bruise half the rosemary. Put in a wide shallow dish with the olive oil and four of the garlic cloves, lightly crushed. Place the chicken breasts on a board and flatten with a mallet or rolling pin. Place in the flavoured olive oil so that they are thoroughly coated. Leave to stand in the fridge overnight. Put the butter, the remaining rosemary leaves, the cayenne pepper and the rest of the garlic in a processor. Blend to a smooth butter. Grill the marinated chicken breasts over a hot barbecue or under a domestic grill, for 10 minutes each side. They should be crispy on the outside and succulent within. Serve with a crisp green salad, maybe a marinated mushroom salad and the rosemary and garlic butter melting over the breasts. Serves 4.

Breast of Chicken with Crab Sauce

4 chicken breasts, 2 tbsp oil
6 oz (175 gm) hand-picked brown and white crab meat
1 oz (25 gm) flour, 1 oz (25 gm) butter
¼ pt (150 ml) white wine, ¼ pt (150 ml) milk
salt and pepper, pinch of cayenne pepper
pinch of grated nutmeg
1 tbsp tomato purée, 1 tbsp lemon juice

Make sure all the bones are removed from the chicken breasts. Arrange them in a shallow roasting tin, brush with the oil and season with salt, pepper and cayenne pepper. Place in a hot oven gas 8/450f/230c and roast for 15 minutes. By this stage they should be cooked but still moist. Meanwhile make the sauce. Melt the butter in a saucepan. Add the flour and cook gently for 2-3 minutes. Don't allow the flour to brown. Whisking all the time add the milk and white wine. Cook until a thick sauce develops. Add more salt and pepper and cayenne pepper, the grated nutmeg, tomato purée, lemon juice and the crab meat. Stir well into the sauce. Add the pan juices from the chicken. If the sauce is too thick add a drop more milk. Serve the sauce with the chicken. Goes well with pasta or new buttery potatoes. Serves 4.

ISLE OF WIGHT WINE

The first attempt to start a vineyard on the Island was in 1793 on the sunny slopes of St Lawrence undercliff. Initially it seemed an ideal spot. Unfortunately the salty spray from the sea remorselessly damaged the vines and grapes, resulting in an inferior wine. Perseverance didn't pay and the attempt was given up thirteen years later.

There are now three commercial vineyards on the

Island. Hamstead, the award winning Barton Manor and Adgeston. Adgeston vineyard has been producing wine since 1970 two years after planting in 1968. It is a delicious fruity wine, with slightly German characteristics. It marries well with local seafoods and all white meats. Barton Manor has strong Royal connections. Queen Victoria and Prince Albert made Barton their home farm and had the medieval farm buildings replaced with modern ones. In 1902 Edward VII gave Osborne to the nation but kept Barton Manor. It was eventually sold into private hands in 1922. The vineyard now offers six quality table wines, including a bottle fermented sparkling wine and an-oak aged wine.

Chicken with Island Wine and Grape Sauce

For this dish I recommend that you use the baby spring chickens.

4 baby chickens
8 oz (225 gm) white grapes
1 pt (570 ml) Island white wine
2 tbsp fresh tarragon
1 level tbsp cornflour, 1 oz (25 gm) butter
2 cloves of garlic, crushed in some salt
lots of freshly ground black pepper

Place the baby chickens in a roasting pan. Pour over the wine and sprinkle with tarragon, crushed garlic and black pepper. Cover with foil and oven bake for 60 minutes.

Test that the chickens are cooked through. If they aren't cook for a little longer. Remove the chickens from the roasting pan and keep warm. Remove the skins and hook out the pips from the grapes if they aren't seedless (fiddly but worth it). Put the pan with all its juices on a ring and raise the heat. Mix the cornflour with a drop of water or wine and stir into the juices. Cook, stirring all the time until the sauce has thickened. Add the grapes, then the butter to enrich the sauce. Cook for a further 4-5 minutes, which will be just long enough to heat the grapes through without over-cooking them. Serve the chickens and the sauce with rice and green beans. Serves 4.

Turkey Breasts with Garlic Bread Sauce

A great deal of poultry is reared on the Isle of Wight including turkeys and geese. If you shop in a small local butcher the chances are you will be buying one of our very own Isle of Wight turkeys.

1 very large or 2 small turkey breasts
2 oz (50 gm) garlic butter
1 onion, finely chopped
3 slices of crustless white bread
4 plump cloves of garlic, 1 bay leaf
pinch of nutmeg, 1 tbsp dry sherry
½ pt (275 ml) milk or single cream for a richer sauce
salt and black pepper
½ pt (275 ml) giblets gravy

Smear the turkey breasts with the garlic butter and put to roast in a moderately hot oven gas 6/400f/200c for 60 minutes. In a saucepan put the onion, bread (broken into pieces), whole garlic cloves, bay leaf, nutmeg, sherry and milk or cream. Simmer gently for 30 minutes. Remove the bay leaf, purée the sauce, season to taste and keep warm until ready to serve. Carve the turkey which should be juicy and not dry. Arrange down the centre of each plate. Pour some garlic sauce down one side of the turkey slices and hot giblets gravy down the other side. Serve with traditional Christmas vegetables. Serves 4.

Rabbits (then called Coney) were first introduced to the Island in 1225. Bowcombe Manor even employed a keeper of conies who successfully sold around 200 skins per year. Coney-garths (stone walled enclosures) were built at Bowcombe and on many other estates to keep the burrowing rabbits in. By the 15th century they were so profitable that rabbit groves were taken into account when land leases were granted. Inevitably the Island became over-run and little was done to check their numbers until 1845 when foxes were introduced for sporting purposes.

Bowcombe Manor Rabbit Pie

If you are using wild rabbit for any of these recipes you may wish to blanch it first. Place the rabbit in a saucepan of cold water. Bring it to the boil then remove the rabbit and plunge immediately into cold water.

> *8 oz (225 gm) short pastry made with 8 oz (225 gm)*
> *plain flour, 2 tspn celery salt, 2 oz (50 gm) butter or*
> *margarine and 3 oz (75 gm) lard*
> *1 plump rabbit or 2 small ones*
> *4 thinly sliced tomatoes*
> *4 tbsp chopped parsley*
> *8 oz (225 gm) rindless bacon rashers*
> *4 tbsp freshly chopped parsley*
> *the grated rind of 1 lemon*
> *lots of black pepper*
> *pinch of salt depending on how salty the bacon*

Chop the rabbit into small joints. Arrange in layers in a deep pie dish with the tomatoes, bacon, parsley, salt and pepper. Top with the shortcrust pastry and make a hole in the top. Put in a preheated oven gas 4/350f/180c for 2 hours. After the first hour lightly cover the top of the pie with greaseproof paper. This will prevent the pastry from scorching. Serve the pie piping hot with parsley sauce and new potatoes. Serves 4.

N.B. This pie is equally delicious served cold. Finish off by making up ¼ pt (150 ml) good flavoured stock with 2 tspn of gelatine dissolved in it, then pour into the hole in the centre of the pie. Chill, then serve with crisp salad and green tomato pickle.

Rabbit with Spring Vegetables and Chive Sauce

2 small, jointed rabbits
1 oz (25 gm) flour, 1 oz (25 gm) butter
½ pt (275 ml) white wine
½ pt (275 ml) chicken stock
4 oz (110 gm) scrubbed baby carrots
4 oz (110 gm) Kenya beans, cut into 2 inch lengths
4 oz (110 gm) peas
4 oz (110 gm) asparagus, trimmed and cut
into 2 inch lengths, ½ red pepper, cut into small dice
4 tbsp chopped fresh chives
salt and pepper, 2 tbsp double cream

Melt the butter in a pan large enough to take all the ingredients. Add the flour and cook gently for a couple of minutes. Do not allow to brown. Whisking all the time add the wine and chicken stock. Simmer gently until a sauce forms. Add the carrots and the rabbit and simmer gently for 30 minutes. Then add the remaining vegetables, chives and cream and simmer for 10 more minutes or until all the vegetables are tender. Season to taste. Serve with rice or new boiled potatoes. Serves 4.

Rabbit Casserole with Whole Grain Mustard

4 plump rabbit legs
8 baby carrots, well scrubbed
4 shallots or 1 onion, finely chopped
2 cloves of garlic
½ pt (275 ml) medium white wine
1 chicken stock cube, dissolved in ½ pt (275 ml) water
small bunch of chopped fresh chives
1 small yellow pepper, finely diced
1 heaped tbsp I.O.W whole grain mustard
1 heaped tbsp seasoned flour
2 tbsp double cream, 2 oz (50 gm) butter
some oil, cornflour

Toss the rabbit legs in seasoned flour then brown in a frying pan in the oil. Take out of the pan and put to one side. In a clean pan put some more oil and soften the onions and crushed garlic. Add the white wine, stock, and cream and simmer rapidly for 10 minutes. To this sauce add the rabbit and carrots and simmer gently for 20 minutes. (Rabbit doesn't take long to cook). Now look at the sauce. If it is too thin, thicken with 2 tspn of cornflour mixed with a drop of milk and stir into the casserole while it is still cooking. Now add the diced pepper and the mustard and simmer gently for five more minutes. N.B: mustard looses its spicy flavour if overheated. Now add the butter for extra richness. Serve this dish with Basmati rice. Contrary to all the rules, I like my Basmati rice to be a little sticky with this dish, I therefore stir the rice while it is cooking. Garnish with heaps of chopped chives. Serves 4.

The hare is indigenous to the Island, with a long season that lasts from August to February. Its dark meat has a rather unique flavour. Rich and gamey yet low in fat.

Haunch of Hare with Sage Sauce

4 legs (haunches) of hare
8 rashers of streaky bacon
oil, 2 tbsp flour
1 large onion, finely sliced
3 cloves of garlic, crushed in a little salt
½ pt (275 ml) red wine or beer
½ pt (275 ml) beef stock
the blood from the hare
1 tbsp tomato purée
1 tbsp dried sage (in this recipe, better than fresh)
black pepper

Wrap the streaky bacon around the hare, two rashers per joint, then toss the hare in the flour and brown in the oil. Put into a casserole dish. Add the onion to the same pan with a drop more oil if required and fry until a pale golden brown. Add the rest of the ingredients and bring to the boil stirring all the time. Pour the sauce over the hare and place the casserole in the oven and bake slowly gas 4/350f/180c for 2 hours. Test the hare after one and a half hours to see if it is cooked as over-cooked hare can become a little dry.

Serve with buttered noodles. Serves 4.

Saddle of Hare with Cobnut and Prune Sauce

A relative of the hazelnut, cobnuts are sold fresh in many small local greengrocers during the autumn.

2 saddles of hare
4 rashers of streaky bacon
1 onion finely chopped
the blood from the hare
½ pt (275 ml) strong beef stock
½ pt (275 ml) Guinness
1 level tbsp cornflour
2 sprigs of rosemary
2 sprigs of thyme
2 cloves of garlic, crushed with a little salt
black pepper
4 oz (110 gm) dried chopped prunes
4 oz (110 gm) shelled fresh cobnuts

Lay the rashers of bacon over the saddles and secure with cocktail sticks. Place in a roasting tin and cook in a hot oven gas 7/425f/220c for 30-40 minutes. When tested a delicate pale pink juice should exude from the skewered hole. (Saddle of hare is best served pink). Meanwhile make the sauce. Soften the onion in the oil until golden brown. Add the rosemary, thyme, prunes, garlic and nuts. Then add the stock and Guinness. Raise the heat and simmer the sauce for 30 minutes. Remove the hare from the oven and put to one side to rest. Pour the sauce from the saucepan into the roasting pan to collect up all the juices. Stir together. Mix the cornflour with a drop of cold water and add to the sauce, stirring continuously. Carve the saddle of hare and serve with the sauce. Accompany with mashed swede, sprouts and game chips. Serves 4.

The Pepper Pot Lighthouse, St Catherine's Down

WOOD PIGEON

Because the land on the Island is mainly put to arable farming it attracts thousands of wood pigeons every year. Wood pigeon can do a great deal of damage to crops, and are fair game. Hence they are readily available at an incredibly low price in local shops. Normally sold on the feather, they are however, one of the easiest birds to pluck. In the main they eat the Island's barley which gives them a good flavour. Wild pigeon has a dark, strong tasting meat that needs a good flavoursome sauce to go with it.

75

Wood Pigeon and Mussel Pie

8 oz (225 gm) rough puff pastry
the flesh of 3 wood pigeon
1 kilo of mussels
1 coarsely sliced onion
2 sliced carrots
pinch of freshly ground nutmeg
pinch of cayenne pepper
grated rind of an orange
½ pt (275 ml) red wine
2 tbsp flour salt and pepper

First prepare the mussels. Scrub thoroughly and remove the black beards. Place in a large saucepan, seal tightly with the lid and place on the highest heat or flame of your cooker. Shake the saucepan around but make sure it never leaves the heat. After eight minutes remove the lid and start removing the mussels that have opened. Continue to do this until all the mussels have been removed. Discard any mussels that after 15 minutes refuse to open. Take the mussels from the shells and reserve with any juice that has escaped. Toss the pigeon meat in the flour then layer the meat, mussels and vegetables and flavourings in a deep pie dish. Season with salt and lots of black pepper. Pour over the red wine. Roll out the pastry and cover the pie. Make a small incision in the centre. Then put on a baking sheet, then into a preheated oven gas 4/350f/180c and bake for 2 hours. After the first hour loosely cover the pie with greaseproof paper to prevent the pastry from scorching. Serves 4.

Wood Pigeon with Sloe Gin Sauce

4 plump pigeons
1 onion or 4 shallots, finely chopped
½ pt (275 ml) stock made from the pigeon bones
¼ pt (150 ml) sloe gin
1 tbsp of any herb jelly
1 tspn tomato purée
2 tspn cornflour
lots of freshly ground black pepper, salt

First prepare the pigeons. Remove the legs, then take a sharp knife and split the breasts away from the carcass by cutting in half through the cavity. You should end up with the two breasts attached to the breast bone on one half and the back bone of the bird on the other half. Put the back bone and legs in a saucepan with onions, carrots and your favourite spices. Simmer gently for a couple of hours to make the stock. Place the four pairs of breasts, still connected to the bone, in a roasting tin and smear liberally with butter. Put in a preheated oven gas 5/190c/375f for 15-20 minutes depending on how well you like them cooked i.e. rare or pink. Well-done roast pigeon will become tough roast pigeon. Meanwhile make the sauce. Soften the onion and lightly brown in a small amount of oil. Add the now strained stock, sloe gin, herb jelly, tomato purée and black peppercorns. Simmer rapidly until reduced by half. Mix the cornflour with a drop of water and add to the sauce. Simmer until thickened. Add the meat juices from the roast pigeon. Season to taste. Either serve the two breasts still on the bone or carefully remove, slice each one in half to form two petals and fan out onto hot plates. Then pour the sauce around the breasts. Serve with creamed potato and braised red cabbage. Serves 4.

Wild Duck with Wild Elderberries

Duck and elderberries come into season almost at the same time, though elderberries are far more prolific than the wild duck.

4 duck breasts
4 oz (110 gm) elderberries
1 oz (25 gm) castor sugar
1 inch piece of root ginger, peeled and grated
½ pt (275 ml) stock from the duck carcasses or
chicken cube, 1 tbsp soya sauce
1 small glass of port
1 onion, finely chopped
oil, 1 level tbsp cornflour
salt and pepper

Remove the breasts from the ducks. Put some oil in a frying pan and place the duck breasts, skin side down in the pan. Fry very gently on as low a temperature as possible for 15 minutes. Turn over and cook for a further 5 minutes. It is essential that the breasts are not over-cooked or they will become tough.

To make the sauce. Soften the onion in a little oil. Add the elderberries, sugar, ginger, chicken stock, soya sauce and port. Simmer for 20 minutes. Mix the cornflour with a drop of cold water and then add to the sauce. Stir continuously until the sauce thickens. Add the pan juices from the duck. Carve the duck into thin slices and serve with the sauce. Serves 4.

Pheasant in Godshill Barn Cider with Apple Cakes

In the thirteenth century cider-making took place at Wootton Manor. Today a good strong cider can be bought at the Cider Barn in Godshill along with their many English country wines.

2 small hen pheasants
1 pt (570 ml) Godshill dry cider
8 shallots, 4 cloves of garlic, crushed in salt
2 tspn dried basil or sage
1 chicken stock cube, oil, 1 tbsp cornflour

Put some oil in a large pan and brown the pheasants all over. Take out and put to one side. Skin the shallots, keep whole and lightly brown in the same pan. Add the garlic and cook until pale and golden. Now add the crumbled stock cube, cider, and herbs. Simmer for a couple of minutes to amalgamate the flavours. Place the pheasants in an oven-proof casserole dish. Pour over the cider sauce. Cover with a lid or tin foil and cook in a preheated oven gas 4/180c/350f for 1 hour 30 minutes. Remove the pheasants from the casserole and keep warm. Mix the cornflour with a drop of water then add to the sauce that the pheasants have been cooking in. Put on the hob and simmer until the sauce thickens. If the dish is not heat proof you will have to transfer the sauce to a saucepan. A drop of cream could be added to enrich the sauce. To serve, remove the legs, and carve the breast meat. Arrange on top of the apple cakes. Serves 4.

Apple Cakes
1 large crisp dessert apple
1 medium potato, salt and pepper
1 level tspn dried sage, ½ beaten egg

Grate the apple and potato. Mix together with the season-ing, sage and beaten egg. Heat some oil in a frying pan. Drop in spoonfuls of the mixture and cook slowly for 10 minutes. Turn over and cook slowly on the other side for a further 10 minutes. The cakes can be pre-cooked and reheated.

Pheasant with Wild Chestnut Sauce

1 large or 2 small pheasants
2 oz (50 gm) butter
4 rashers of streaky bacon
8 oz (225 gm) peeled chestnuts
1 diced carrot, 1 small chopped onion
½ pt (275 ml) chicken stock
¼ pt (150 ml) medium dry sherry
1 small clove of garlic, 1 tspn castor sugar
½ tspn cinnamon, ½ tspn cayenne pepper
½ tspn dried thyme, salt and black pepper

Smear the butter over the pheasants then lay the rashers of bacon over the breast. Place in a roasting pan on its side and roast for 20 minutes. Turn the pheasant onto its other side and roast for a further 20 minutes. Meanwhile make the sauce. Put the carrot and onion in a saucepan with some oil and cook gently for 10 minutes. Add the rest of the ingredients and simmer until the chestnuts are soft. Put the sauce into a blender and whiz until smooth. Pour back into the saucepan. Pour in any meat juices from the roast pheasant. Thin the sauce if necessary with a drop of stock, water or sherry. Season to taste. Carve the pheasant and serve with the sauce. N.B. 2 tbsp of cream can be added to the sauce to enrich it. Serves 4.

The remains of deer bones have been found on archaeological digs of the Island's Roman villas. During the Middle Ages, both red and fallow deer were hunted in Parkhurst Forest and Borthwood. Today the only deer on the Island have been deliberately introduced. A good place to see them is along the Stenbury trail that runs behind Appuldurcombe House.

Venison Burgers with Peppercorn Sauce

This is ideal for the cheaper off-cuts of venison and great for barbecues. The recipe below makes quarter-pound burgers. Double the quantities for half-pounders and cook five minutes longer on each side.

> *1 lb (450 gm) shoulder of venison*
> *1 small onion, coarsely chopped*
> *1 small beaten egg*
> *1 tspn crushed juniper berries*
> *2 tspn dried sage*
> *1 thin slice of bread*
> *salt and lots of black pepper*

Dice the venison and put in a processor with the rest of the ingredients. Whiz until blended but still retaining a coarse texture. Mould the mixture into four burger shapes and put in the fridge until ready to grill or fry. Fry in medium hot shallow fat for approximately 8 minutes each side or longer for a well-done burger. If barbecuing, remember to oil the rack before cooking the burgers. Again grill for about 8 minutes each side but watch them all the time to avoid too much burning on the outside. Serves 4.

Venison Casserole with Pearl Barley and Satsumas

1 ½ lb (700 gm) shoulder or haunch of venison
seasoned flour, oil for frying
1 large onion, finely sliced
2 cloves of garlic
2 tspn dried basil
4 satsumas
½ pt (275 ml) red wine
½ pt (275 ml) beef or venison stock
2 oz (50 gm) pearl barley
1 tbsp tomato purée
1 tspn crushed juniper berries
1 tspn cumin seeds
salt and black pepper, 2 tspn sugar

Cut the venison into 1 inch cubes. Toss in the seasoned flour. In small batches, fry the cubes of venison in hot oil until golden. Take out of the frying pan and put into a casserole dish with the whole satsumas. In the same frying pan add more oil and fry the onions until golden brown. Add the garlic, basil, cumin seeds, crushed juniper berries, pearl barley and sugar. Quickly stir around and then add the stock, red wine and tomato purée. Season with the salt and pepper then pour over the venison. Seal tightly with a lid or tin foil and cook in the oven, gas 4/350f/180c for approximately 2 hours. After 90 minutes check the casserole to see if the meat is already nice and tender (an over-cooked casserole can leave the meat tasteless because all the flavour has escaped into the sauce). Also check that it hasn't become too dry with the absorption of the pearl barley. If it has add a drop more stock or water. This is a hearty dish and I like to serve it with a watercress and orange salad and crusty bread. Serves 4.

Venison Cutlets with Celeriac Sauce

This is an unusual sauce to serve with venison. The contrasting flavour of celeriac makes a perfect marriage.

8 cutlets taken from the saddle
4 rashers of streaky bacon
1 large celeriac
1 small potato, peeled and halved
juice of 1 lemon
2 cloves of garlic, crushed in a little salt
1 inch fresh horseradish root, finely grated
¼ pt (150 ml) double cream
1 tspn of celery salt and black pepper

Stretch the rashers of bacon, cut in half and wrap around the venison cutlets. Pan fry for 8 minutes each side. They are best cooked pink. Meanwhile make the sauce (it can be made in advance). Peel the celeriac, cut into cubes and boil in plenty of salted water with the potato and lemon juice. Drain and put in a blender with the rest of the sauce ingredients. Blend to a smooth purée. Serve immediately with the venison cutlets. Accompany with redcurrant jelly, and braised red cabbage or baby beetroot. Serves 4.

Steak and Oyster Puff

This is a quick version of Steak and Oyster Pie. It was typical in the past to enhance the flavour of meat with fish. Anchovies were another popular flavouring in traditional English meat cookery.

12 oz (350 gm) fillet or sirloin steak, cut into 1 inch cubes
1 tbsp seasoned flour
12-16 fresh Newtown oysters
1 lb (450 gm) puff pastry or 4 jumbo vol au vents
1 large onion, finely chopped
½ pt (275ml) strong beef stock
2 tbsp soya sauce
dash Worcester sauce
1 tspn green peppercorns (optional)
3-4 cloves of garlic, crushed in salt
1 tbsp corn flour
freshly chopped parsley or coriander, oil

First prepare the pastry boxes. Roll out the puff pastry to ¼ inch thick for bought pastry and ½ inch thick for homemade pastry. Cut into four oblongs about 4 inches by 3 inches. Then with a sharp knife cut another oblong ½ inch inside the pastry shape. Be careful not to cut right through to the bottom. Place on a lightly oiled baking sheet. Carefully brush with beaten egg. Don't allow the egg to seep between the inner cut or it will glue the cut edge back together again. Bake in a hot oven gas 7/425f/230c for 10 minutes or until golden brown.

Meanwhile make the filling. Remove the oysters from their shells. Do this over a bowl to catch the juices. (Be very careful. Use a rigid knife – preferably an oyster knife – and protect your hands with a tea towel). Put the oysters and their juices to one side. Soften the onion and garlic in a frying pan. Toss the steak in the seasoned flour and add to the pan and fry until golden. You may need a little more oil. Raise the heat under the pan and add the Worcester sauce, soya sauce, juice from the oysters, the green peppercorns and the stock. Simmer rapidly to reduce the sauce. Avoid over cooking the steak. Mix the cornflour with a drop of cold water and add to the sauce. Continue cooking until the sauce is thick. Five minutes before serving add the fresh oysters (they should be heated through but not over-cooked). Spoon the mixture into the warm pre-prepared pastry boxes with the sea-scented sauce and garnish with chopped parsley or coriander. Serves 4.

Appley Tower, Ryde

Char-Grilled Steak with Garlic and Sun-dried Tomato Butter

4 fillet steaks 7-8 oz (195-225 gm) in weight
oil
salt and pepper
4 oz (110 gm) cubed butter
4 cloves of garlic
2 tbsp parsley
6 sun-dried tomatoes in herb oil

First make the butter. Put the butter, garlic, parsley and sun-dried tomatoes in a blender and whiz until smooth. Take out of the blender and arrange in a long thin line on a piece of greaseproof paper. Roll up into a sausage shape and chill. Before serving the steaks, the chilled butter should be cut into discs.

Smear the steaks with oil and season both sides with plenty of black pepper but only a small amount of salt. When the coals on the barbecue are white put the steak over the hottest part, watching all the time. Grill for 8 minutes on each side. If they begin to burn early on move them to the cooler edges. If you like your steaks well-done cook them 10 minutes each side. If you are offering your guests a choice (though I personally would avoid this) put the steaks that are to be well-done on to cook first.

Alternative method for cooking indoors: heat some oil in a pan then brown the steaks on each side, this should take no more than 2 minutes. Place the steaks on a baking tray and place them in a hot preheated oven gas 9/475f/240c and bake for 10 minutes or 15 minutes for well done steaks. Put some discs of tomato butter on top of the steaks so that they melt over the meat and serve with salad and baked potatoes. Serves 4.

LAMB

As early as the 14th century the Island was a major producer of lamb. Production reached its zenith in the late 18th century when turnips were first grown, thus producing winter fodder. As many as 40,000 sheep were shorn for wool export each year and by the 1800's as many as 1,000 sheep per week were being sent to mainland markets.

It wasn't until much later that dairy cattle were kept on the Island. Before that most of the milk and cheese came from sheep milk. In the late 18th century a cheese called 'Isle of Wight Rock' was produced - though it was considered unpalatable and supposedly required a sledgehammer to cut it.

From April to September I only ever cook lamb that needs a short burst of heat under the grill, over a barbecue or in a frying pan. From October to March lamb tends to be less tender, and requires longer, slower cooking.

Lamb Cutlets with Orange and Laverbread Sauce

Laverbread is a puréed seaweed and gives a faintly fishy taste to this dish.

8 lamb cutlets, oil
1 large onion, skinned and quartered
the juice and finely grated rind of 1 orange
1 level tbsp cornflour
1 pt (570 ml) strong, preferably gelatinous, chicken or lamb stock
1 tbsp tinned or frozen laverbread
2 tbsp double cream
salt and lots of black pepper

First prepare the sauce. Put the orange rind, orange juice, onion and stock in a saucepan. Simmer until the onion is soft and the stock is reduced by half. Put into a blender and whiz until smooth. Return to the saucepan and add the laverbread and double cream. Mix the cornflour with a drop of water and add to the sauce. Stirring all the time bring to the boil. Season with salt and pepper.

Smear the lamb cutlets with oil and grill or pan fry for 5 minutes each side. Serve with the sauce, garnished with a thin slice of orange and a sprig of watercress. Accompany with French beans and new potatoes. Serves 4.

Neck of Lamb with Asparagus Tips

2 lb (900 gm) neck fillet of lamb
oil for frying
2 tbsp seasoned flour
2 sprigs of fresh thyme leaves
small bunch of fresh basil leaves
½ pt (275 ml) white wine
juice of 2 lemons
8 oz (225 gm) asparagus tips (the stalks can be used to
make soup)
2 egg yolks
salt and pepper

Cut the lamb fillet into chunks. Toss lightly in the flour, shaking off any excess, and sâuté in hot oil until golden brown. Add the herbs, wine and all but 1 tbsp of lemon juice. Cover the pan and cook gently for 1 hour, maybe a little more, until the meat is tender.

Meanwhile sâuté the asparagus tips in more oil until they are tender. Add the asparagus, oil and lemon juice to the lamb and simmer for about 5 minutes.

Stir the egg yolks together and add 4 tbsp of the cooking stock to them. Take the casserole off the heat and stir the yolk mixture into the casserole. Return to the heat for about five minutes to thicken the sauce. It is however essential that the sauce doesn't boil or it will curdle. Serve with petit pois and buttered noodles. Serves 4.

Leg of Spring Lamb with Creamy Lemon and Mint Sauce

I first served this dish in my tiny back-street restaurant over fourteen years ago. It has always been a tremendous success and I have resurrected it many times since.

1 leg of lamb approximately 3 lb (1.4 kg) in weight
1 lemon, cut into thin slices
1 tbsp runny honey
oil, 2 oz (50 gm) butter
1 level tbsp plain flour
½ pt (275 ml) chicken stock
the juice and grated rind of 1 lemon
1 small tub of soured cream
2 tbsp chopped fresh mint, salt and pepper

Put the leg of lamb in a roasting pan. Arrange the lemon slices on top and dribble over the runny honey. Roast gas 6/400f/200c for approximately 1 hour 15 minutes, longer if you like your lamb well done. To test pierce the joint with a skewer, the juice that exudes from the hole should run clear.

Meanwhile make the sauce. Put the butter in a saucepan and add the flour. Cook for a couple of minutes without browning. Stirring all the time add the stock, lemon juice and lemon rind. Cook until thickened then lower the heat and gently simmer for 15 minutes to extract the flavour from the lemon rind.

Remove the lamb from the oven and put to one side to rest. Tip the pan juices into the sauce then add the chopped mint and the soured cream. Simmer for 5 minutes. Carve the meat and serve with the sauce. Accompany with broad beans and sâuté of new potatoes. Serves 4.

Loin of Pork with Caper and Paprika Sauce

I acquired this recipe more than eighteen years ago from the now retired Mr Alan Smith, the popular and highly respected owner of Melville Hall Hotel, Sandown. I can remember him being very proud of what was then an innovative recipe. He used to serve it with veal escalopes but is also goes beautifully with pork. In the 1800's many smallholdings sprung up all over the Island. Nearly all of them reared pigs – large porkers with black spots (Gloucester Old Spots) were the favourite breed.

4 large chunky pork loin chops
oil
1 onion, very finely chopped
2 cloves of garlic, crushed in a little salt
1 level tbsp tomato purée
1 tbsp capers
1 tbsp hot paprika
½ pt (275 ml) white wine
½ pt (275 ml) double cream

Soften the onion and garlic in 2 tbsp oil, don't allow to brown. Add the paprika and cook for a couple of minutes to take away the rawness of the spice. Add the tomato purée, capers and wine. Simmer rapidly to reduce by half.

Put the chops to grill, fry or barbecue, 8 minutes each side or 10 minutes for crispy chops.

Add the cream to the reduced sauce and simmer until the sauce thickens. Season to taste and serve with the pork chops. Accompany with broccoli and sâuté potatoes. Serves 4.

Nuggets of Pork with Apple, Sage and Onion Relish

2 large or 3 small fillets of pork, cut into 2 inch thick discs
1 large onion, finely chopped
1 tbsp oil
1 oz (25 gm) butter
2 peeled and diced cooking apples
1 tbsp castor sugar
1 tbsp freshly chopped sage
oil for frying
¼ pt (150 ml) white wine or chicken stock
1 oz (25 gm) cold butter
salt and pepper

First make the relish. Melt the butter and 1 tbsp oil in a saucepan. Add the onion and cook slowly until the onion is soft. Add the apple, chopped sage and sugar. Cover the pan with a lid and simmer until the apple has reduced to a pulp. Beat with a fork to blend the ingredients together. Put to one side and keep warm. This sauce can be made in advance and reheated or served cold with cold roast pork.

Heat some oil in a frying pan and add the nuggets of pork. Sâuté for 5 minutes each side, until golden and slightly crunchy on the surface. Push the pork to one side and add the wine and butter. Bring to the boil so that a thin glaze forms. Serve the pork immediately. Coat with a little of the glaze and put a spoonful of relish on the side. Serves 4.

PUDDINGS, CAKES AND
AFTERNOON TEAS

There's nothing quite like an English strawberry, and thanks to its mild climate and fertile soil, particularly in the Arreton Valley, the Island has the longest growing season in England – occasionally lasting into December.

Self-pick strawberry farms can be found all over the Island, often open in April right through to November. Holiday-makers can look forward to that universal Southern English treat, 'strawberries and cream' made from strawberries that seem riper, sweeter, more tender, fruitier, and juicier than anywhere else.

Strawberry Ice Cream

1½ lb (700 gm) ripe strawberries
6-8 oz (175-225 gm) castor sugar
(more for a softer ice cream)
1 pt (570 ml) double cream
3 large eggs, separated
1 tbsp fresh lemon juice

Purée the strawberries and push through a fine hair sieve to remove the tiny pips. Add the lemon juice to the strawberry purée. Put the egg yolks and half the sugar in a bowl over a saucepan of boiling water. Whisk until thick, pale and creamy. Cool. Whisk the cream to peaks. Whisk the egg white into peaks. Add the remaining sugar to the egg whites and whisk until stiff. Fold the now cold egg yolk mixture into the whipped cream. Then fold in the strawberry purée. Finally fold in the egg whites. Pour into a shallow container and freeze. If the ice cream freezes too hard to serve, transfer to the fridge half an hour before serving. Serves 4 – 6.

Strawberry Shortcake

A simple sweet to make yet because it is – and must be – made with butter it carries a flavour of some sophistication. Best eaten the same day it is made. Serve in the afternoon with a refreshing cup of Earl Grey tea.

8 oz (225 gm) ripe strawberries
clotted or whipped double cream
icing sugar

Shortcake
6 oz (175 gm) good quality butter
6 oz (175 gm) castor sugar
3 eggs, 1 tsp vanilla essence
8 oz (225 gm) self raising flour

Cream together butter and sugar until soft, pale and fluffy. Add vanilla essence. Gradually add the beaten eggs. Add a teaspoon of flour with each addition of egg to prevent curdling (this shouldn't be necessary if the butter is soft enough). Sift the flour, then carefully fold into the creamed mixture. This mixture is quite firm, unlike a sponge mix, so don't be tempted to add any liquid; and don't overwork or the air will be removed. Divide the mixture between two lightly greased and floured 7 inch sandwich tins. Level the mixture then bake in the centre of a moderate oven gas 4/180c/350f for 25-30 minutes. Cool before turning out. When completely cold, sandwich together with the whipped or clotted cream and sliced strawberries. Dredge with fine icing sugar. Serves 6 – 8.

Strawberry Chocolate Fondue

A simple pudding for four and perfect if you're caught on the hop.

8 oz (225 gm) dark quality chocolate
1 oz (25 gm) best butter
¼ pt (150 ml) double or whipping cream
1 tbsp brandy
1 lb (450 gm) top quality strawberries

Break up the chocolate and put in a heavy bottomed, preferably non-stick saucepan with the cream. Heat very gently until the chocolate has melted and a thick chocolate sauce has been achieved. Stir in the butter and the brandy. Arrange the strawberries around the edge of individual plates. Put a ramekin dish or similar in the centre of the strawberries and pour the chocolate fondue into these little dishes. Serve immediately before the chocolate cools. To avoid messy fingers use little dessert forks to hold the strawberries while dipping them into the sauce.

Bembridge Mill

Coconut Mousse with Strawberry Sauce

Coconut and strawberries are an unusual but inspired blend.

14 oz (400 gm) can of condensed milk
8 oz (225 gm) desiccated coconut
small tub Greek, strained yoghurt
1 sachet gelatine
3 egg whites
8 oz (225 gm) strawberries
3 oz (75 gm) castor sugar

Blend the coconut and the condensed milk together. Stand for 1 hour to soften the coconut. Sprinkle the gelatine over 3 tbsp cold water. Stand a few minutes until swollen then heat in a double saucepan or in a microwave until the crystals are dissolved. Whisk the egg whites to stiff peaks. Add the yoghurt to the coconut flavoured milk. Then quickly beat in the softened gelatine. Mix quickly before the gelatine has a chance to form strings. (Keeping the coconut mixture at room temperature will help to avoid this problem). Fold in the beaten egg white and pour into individual or one large dish, that will look pretty when the mousse is turned out.

Strawberry sauce: Put the sugar in a saucepan with a scant ¼ pt (150 ml) water. Dissolve the sugar then simmer rapidly for 5 minutes. Put the strawberries in a blender. Pour over the hot syrup and process to a smooth sauce. Push through a fine sieve to remove the tiny pips. Taste and add a dash of lemon juice if necessary.

Turn out the mousse/s. Pour the sauce around and garnish with more strawberries. Serves 8.

Strawberry and Lemon Roulade with Rose-Scented Sauce

A stupendous dinner party dessert, or serve with after-noon tea on the lawn.

3 large eggs, 4 oz (110 gm) castor sugar
3 oz (75 gm) ground almonds
½ oz (10 gm) fine cake or digestive biscuit crumbs

Filling and Sauce
½ pt (275 ml) double cream
1 tbsp lemon curd, 1 lb (450 gm) strawberries
1 tbsp triple distilled rosewater
3-4 oz (75-110 gm) castor sugar

Line a Swiss roll tin with buttered greaseproof paper and scatter finely with the cake crumbs. Whisk together the eggs and sugar until thick and creamy. Very gently fold in the ground almonds. Spread this mixture evenly, over the Swiss roll tin. Bake near the top of the oven for 12 minutes, gas 5/190c/375f until just firm. Turn out onto a sheet of paper sprinkled with sugar while still warm. Place another piece of greaseproof paper on top then roll up Swiss roll fashion. (If you don't do this the cake may crack when it is filled with cream and finally rolled up. Some people prefer this effect).

Whip the cream with the lemon curd. Chop half the strawberries and fold into the cream. Unroll the cold sponge and spread with the lemon and strawberry cream. Roll up again and dredge with icing sugar.

To make the sauce, put the sugar in a saucepan with 4 tbsp water and the rosewater. Dissolve the sugar, then simmer rapidly for 5 minutes. Put this syrup with the strawberries in a blender and purée. Sieve out the tiny strawberry pips.

To serve, trim away the coarse ends of the roulade. Cut 1 inch thick slices. Lay in the centre of individual plates. Pour the sauce around and garnish with more strawberries and tiny pink rose petals. Serves 6.

Quick Strawberry Meringue

Serve in pretty, but heat-proof dishes. Children will love it too.

1 lb (450 gm) strawberries, thickly sliced
6 oz (175 gm) castor sugar
2 tbsp Grand Marnier
½ tbsp lemon juice
3 large egg whites

Toss the sliced strawberries in the Grand Marnier, the lemon juice and 2 oz (50 gm) of the sugar. Divide between four dishes. Whisk the egg whites to stiff peaks, then whisk in the remaining castor sugar. Heat the grill. Pile the meringue on top of the strawberries. Place on the grill tray and slide under the grill. Have the dishes as far away from the flame/element as possible. At this stage watch the dessert like a hawk, it burns quickly. As soon as the meringue begins to turn a golden brown colour it is ready to serve. Serves 4.

Strawberry and Elderflower Sorbet

A perfect sweet to mark the beginning of the season of summer fruits. Throughout June the hedgerows are heavy with fragrant elderflower blossoms. Gather the flowers when the umbles are just beginning to bloom and the blossom is creamy white.

1 lb (450 gm) ripe strawberries
8 oz (225 gm) castor sugar
½ pt (275 ml) water
4 sprays of elderflowers
juice of half a lemon
1 egg white

Put the sugar, water and elderflowers in a saucepan. Heat gently until the sugar has dissolved, then raise the heat and boil the sugar syrup for 15 minutes.

Add the strawberries and lemon juice to the syrup and boil for a further 5 minutes. Remove the elderflowers. Puree the fruit and syrup then push through a fine sieve to remove the strawberry pips. Cool, then pour into a plastic container and freeze to a firmish slush (this will take about 2 hours).

Whisk the egg white in a clean bowl. Then working very quickly, take the sorbet from the freezer. Break up with a fork and add to the egg white. Whisk hard or on fast speed for 30 seconds until the sorbet has become light and fluffy. It is essential that you work quickly so that it doesn't melt. Quickly spoon back into its plastic container (its bulk will have increased so you may find you need a larger one) and fast freeze for 1 hour. Leave in the freezer until ready to serve. Because of the egg white you should be able to serve this sorbet straight from the freezer. Serves 4 – possibly more.

Red Berry Jelly with Raspberry Sauce

The Cider Barn at Godshill, as well as cider, has a fascinating range of old English fruit wines.

1 pt (570 ml) strawberry wine
1 lb (450 gm) mixed red berries i.e. raspberries,
strawberries, redcurrants, blackcurrants, blueberries,
loganberries
4 oz (110 gm) castor sugar
1 sachet plus an extra tspn of gelatine

Raspberry sauce
8 oz (225 gm) raspberries
4 oz (110 gm) icing sugar
juice of 1 lemon

Gently heat half of the strawberry wine with the sugar until the sugar has dissolved (don't over heat or it will lose its flavour). Soften the gelatine in 3 tbsp cold water, then heat to dissolve. Stir into the warm sweetened wine. Add the washed fruit to the warm wine, then the remaining cold wine. Pour into a jelly mould. Cover and set in the fridge, preferably overnight.

To make the sauce, put the raspberries, icing sugar and lemon juice into a processor and blend until smooth. Pass through a sieve to remove the raspberry pips. Keep cool until ready to serve.

I like to set the jelly in an oblong terrine then cut thick slices and serve surrounded with the sauce and garnished with extra summer berries.

Queen Victoria spent many months each year at her holiday home Osborne House, and it was well known that she had a sweet tooth and a passion for fresh fruit. Although she was an advocate of seasonal food and always insisted that the best of the season was always on her table even if she never ate it – it gave her pleasure just to see it there – when it came to fruit she seemed to waive this rule. She had several forcing (hot) houses, melon grounds and fruit rooms installed so that she could be supplied with exotic fruit all the year round. Some of her favourites were oranges, grapes, pears and monster apples.

During the summer months she insisted that her luncheon table was always graced with wild strawberries from the woods, (still to be found today) and grapes and raspberries from her kitchen garden.

Norris Castle, East Cowes

Fruits of the Summer Salad with Sweet Damson Wine

There is nothing complicated about this dessert, except the purchasing of fresh fruits that are of pristine quality. The mingling of flavours is delightful.

4 oz (110 gm) each of the following fruits (try and include all the fruits listed to get a good balance of flavours):
English strawberries, raspberries, blackcurrants, redcurrants, blueberries and blackberries
2 oz (50 gm) vanilla sugar
½ pt (275 ml) sweet damson wine from the Cider Barn, Godshill
12 fresh young mint leaves

Carefully wash and dry the fruit (pat with kitchen roll). Slice the strawberries in half or smaller if necessary. Mix the fruits together. Arrange the mint leaves around four sundae glasses so that they poke up above the rims. Spoon the berries into the glasses. Sprinkle evenly with the sugar and then pour over the wine.

I'm not a lover of cream with fresh fruit as I think it dilutes the flavour, however Creme Chantilly for those of you who can't resist is an acceptable accompaniment.

Creme Chantilly (my version)
2 oz (50 gm) coarsely crushed meringue shells
small pot of whipping or double cream

Whisk the cream. Fold in the meringues and serve.

Raspberry Shortbread

10 oz (275 gm) plain flour, 8 oz (225 gm) best butter
4 oz (110 gm) sifted icing sugar
pinch of salt, the yolks of 2 large eggs
2 drops of vanilla essence
8 oz (225 gm) carton of clotted cream
8 oz (225 gm) raspberries, more icing sugar for decoration

Sift the flour with the pinch of salt. Dice the butter and add to the flour. Crumb together. The mixture will become quite soft. Add the icing sugar and stir through. Add the vanilla essence to the egg yolks. Mix, then add to the crumbed mixture. Mix in with a fork and then pull together to form a paste. (A quicker method would be to put all the ingredients in a food mixer and blend until a smooth paste forms).

Divide the pastry in half. Grease two loose-bottomed flan rings. Place on baking trays and press the shortbread into the base of each ring. Flatten with the base of a potato masher. Prick both the pastry bases all over with a fork. To one of the bases only, score – cutting all the way through – six segments. Place both shortbreads in a preheated oven gas 6/400f/ 200c for 20-25 minutes or until golden brown.

When done take out and cool while still in the flan rings. The scored shortbread may have joined together during baking, therefore re-cut through while still warm.

When cold, place the whole ring of shortbread on a serving plate. Whip the clotted cream and spread over the base. Top with the washed and dried raspberries. Arrange the remaining six shortbread sections at a slight angle on top of the raspberries. Accompany with raspberry or strawberry sauce. (See recipe for Red Berry Jelly with Raspberry Sauce). Serves 6.

Gooseberry Fool

There are several ways to make fruit fools. Some recipes suggest a mix of stewed fruit and custard, others half custard, half cream and stewed fruit (my own preferred method) whilst others call for all cream and stewed fruit.

This recipe uses the latter with a small healthy addition of meusli to balance the cream.

8 oz (225 gm) gooseberries
4 oz (110 gm) castor sugar, more if the
gooseberries are tart
½ pt (275 ml) double cream
2 oz (50 gm) muesli, dried fruits picked out

Top and tail the gooseberries. Put in a pan with the castor sugar, tightly seal with a lid and stew 10-15 minutes or until the fruit is soft and pulpy. Mash the fruit, or purée it for a smooth dessert. Chill.

Whip the cream, fold in the muesli and chilled fruit. To serve, pile into glasses and accompany with nutty shortbread biscuits. Serves 4.

Afton Apple Jelly with Blackberry Sauce

Afton Park in Freshwater produces a delicious apple juice, pressed from English Cox and Bramleys, and whose flavour is the secret of this lovely fresh jelly.

1 lb (450 gm) dessert apples
1 pt (570 ml) Afton apple juice
6 oz (175 gm) castor sugar
4 tbsp Calvados
juice of half a lemon
finely pared rind of half a lemon
1½ sachets of gelatine

Blackberry Sauce
8 oz (225 gm) blackberries
4 oz (110 gm) castor sugar
sprig of fresh mint
1 tbsp lemon juice

First make the jelly. Peel and core the apples and cut into dice. Put half the apple juice, the sugar, lemon juice, lemon rind and apples in a saucepan and simmer gently until the sugar has dissolved and the apples are tender.

Soften the gelatine in 3 tbsp of cold apple juice then heat through to dissolve. Add to the apples in the warm juice. Now add the remaining cold juice and the Calvados. Remove the lemon peel then pour into a jelly mould to set overnight. To make the blackberry sauce, put the blackberries, lemon juice, sprig of mint and castor sugar in a saucepan and simmer until the sugar has dissolved and the blackberries are soft and pulpy. Don't over-cook or you will end up with jam. Remove the sprig of mint and pass the fruit through a sieve. Chill before serving.

Turn the jelly into a straight-sided dish and surround with a pool of the blackberry sauce. Serves 6.

Apple and Marzipan Pie with Red Plum Sauce

This is a very simple dessert with a French influence, and a tribute to Isabella de Fortibus, who in the late 13th century was the Island's principal landowner and lived in Carisbrooke Castle.

8 oz (225 gm) puff pastry
6 oz (175 gm) marzipan
2 small or 1 large cooking apple
2 tbsp castor sugar
8 oz (225 gm) red plums
6 oz (175 gm) castor sugar

Divide the pastry in half and roll out two 8 inch circles. Place one onto a baking sheet. Roll out the marzipan to a 7 inch circle then place on top of the pastry circle.

Peel and thinly slice the apple and arrange on top of the marzipan, then sprinkle over the sugar. Dampen the edges of the pastry with the beaten egg and place the remaining circle of puff pastry on top of the apples. Seal down the edges. Brush the whole pie with beaten egg, then mark out a pattern on the surface of the pie with a fork. Bake in a preheated oven gas 7/425f/220c for 35 minutes.

To make the plum sauce, simmer the plums with the sugar until they are pulpy, then pass through a sieve to remove the skins and stones. Serve hot with the pie.

Individual pies can be made in a similar way. They look best when arranged individually on plates in a glistening ruby red puddle of plum sauce. Serves 4.

Rew Valley Cream and Apple Pie

Rew Valley Dairies produce the sort of cream I remember from the days when it used to have flavour and a delicate golden hue.

8 oz (225 gm) biscuit crust pastry made with: 8 oz (225 gm) plain flour, 5 oz (150 gm) butter, 2 oz (50 gm) icing sugar, 1 egg yolk and a scant drop of water

1 lb (450 gm) Cox or Russet apples
4 oz (110 gm) demerara sugar
1 level tspn mixed spice
¼ pt (150 ml) double cream
grated rind of ½ lemon

Roll out half the pastry and line a flan ring. Peel and finely slice the apples and put in a bowl. Add the sugar, mixed spice and lemon rind. Mix well together, then pile into the pastry case, being careful not to damage the pastry.

Roll out the other piece of pastry. Pour the cream over the apples. Top with the remaining pastry, seal the edges and pierce a small hole in the top to allow steam to escape. Sprinkle the surface with icing sugar. Bake immediately in a preheated oven gas 8/450f/230c for 15 minutes then lower the temperature to gas 5/375f/190c for a further 25 minutes. Serve hot or cold with more cream. Serves 4.

Sunshine Apple Flan

I make this dessert simply to celebrate the fact I live on the Isle of Wight. It's very popular with children.

6 oz (175 gm) sweet pastry made with:
6 oz (175 gm) plain flour, 3½ oz (90 gm) butter
1 oz (25 gm) icing
sugar, 1 egg yolk

Mix in a food mixer then chill for 20 minutes before rolling out.

2 small cooking apples
1 orange
2 eggs
4 oz (110 gm) castor sugar
2 ripe peaches

Line a flan ring with the pastry. Finely grate the rind from the orange and squeeze the juice. Peel and core the apple and coarsely grate the flesh. Beat the eggs and add to the grated apple, orange juice, orange rind and castor sugar. Mix well then pour into the pastry case. Bake in a preheated oven gas 8/450f/230c for 10 minutes. Reduce heat to gas 4/350f/180c for a further 30 minutes.

Remove from the oven and cool. Halve the peaches, remove the stones and cut into slices. Arrange in a circle fanning out from the centre of the flan to represent rays from the sun. Serve with slightly sweetened whipped cream. Serves 4 – 6.

Calbourne Classics Lemon and Lime Cheesecake

Calbourne Classics first made their name with a tempting range of ice creams, all of which are made from the milk and cream from their own pedigree Holstein Freisians. They have recently started production of delicious fresh cream desserts, marvellous cheesecakes and rich gateaux. Their lemon and lime cheesecake is a particular favourite of mine.

12 oz (350 gm) cream cheese
½ pt (275 ml) double cream
6 oz (175 gm) castor sugar (more for a less sharp taste)
1 large lemon
1 large plump lime
6 oz (175 gm) ginger biscuits
3 oz (75 gm) butter
1 sachet of gelatine with ½ tspn taken out

Crush the ginger biscuits. Melt the butter and stir into the biscuits. Press this biscuit mixture into the base of a loose-bottomed 7 inch cake tin.

Finely grate the rind from the lemon and the lime and mix into the cream cheese. Add the castor sugar. Squeeze the juice from the lemon and lime and put in a small basin. Sprinkle over the gelatine and wait for it to soften, then heat through to dissolve the crystals. Whip the double cream ready to fold into the cheesecake mixture. When the gelatine is soft quickly beat into the cream cheese, then as it begins to set, fold in the whipped cream. Pour the mixture onto the biscuit base and put in the fridge to set for at least 6 hours.

To remove from the cake tin, run a knife around the sides to loosen then spring the sides to release. Serve with pouring cream. Serves 6.

Lemon and Ginger Syllabub

Syllabub is one of our oldest traditional English desserts and was served all over the country; though it was a luxury only enjoyed by dairy farmers and the landed gentry. The most authentic way to make it is to start the recipe at least 3 days before you intend eating it. The syllabub cream is then spooned into long glasses that are narrow at the bottom, then left to stand. After a few days the liquid will have separated and settled at the bottom of the glass leaving a light foamy cream on the surface.

These days we never seem to have the time to prepare dishes in advance and syllabub has become a rich creamy dessert best served in small portions.

10 fl oz double cream
4 oz (110 gm) castor sugar
juice and finely grated rind of 1 lemon
3 tbsp cream sherry or brandy
1 tbsp chopped crystalized ginger
2 tspn ground ginger

Put the lemon peel, juice, sherry, crystalized ginger, ground ginger and sugar in a bowl. Stir together until the sugar has completely dissolved. Add the cream and whisk until a thick cream forms. Spoon into glasses and refrigerate overnight. (It can however be eaten immediately). Serve with ginger flavoured shortbread biscuits. Serves 4.

Damson Wine Jelly with Poached Pears

A perfect dessert to serve after a delicious winter meal of venison or other game dish.

1 pt (570 ml) Damson wine
a piece of orange peel
1 cinnamon stick
2 blades of mace
4 oz (110 gm) castor sugar
2 tbsp brandy
1 sachet of gelatine crystals
4 ripe pears (but not over ripe)

Peel the pears, leaving the small stems intact. Place in a saucepan with half the wine, the orange peel, cinnamon stick, castor sugar, and mace. Put on a gentle heat and poach until the pears are tender and have absorbed the wine flavour. Remove the pears and chill. Strain the remaining wine.

Soften the gelatine in 3 tbsp cold water, then heat through until dissolved. Add to the poaching liquid, then add the rest of the damson wine and the brandy. Pour into a jelly mould and refrigerate overnight until set. Serve the jelly with the poached pears and cold whipped cream. Serves 4.

Christmas Ice Cream

In recent years an extensive ice-cream industry has developed on the Island. Several small farms are now producing authentic ice-cream for the local population and tourists alike to enjoy. This recipe shows you how to make your own without the aid of an ice-cream maker.

1 pt (570 ml) double cream
4 oz (110 gm) castor sugar
2 eggs, separated, 4 tbsp rum
2 oz (50 gm) glace cherries, 1 oz (25 gm) angelica
1 oz (25 gm) candied peel
1 oz (25 gm) lightly toasted flaked almonds
1 oz (25 gm) chopped pistachio nuts
2 oz (50 gm) sultanas, 1 tspn mixed spice
grated rind and juice of 1 orange
grated rind and juice of 1 lemon
½ tspn vanilla essence

Chop the glace cherries and angelica into tiny pieces. Put the sultanas, orange juice and rind, lemon juice and rind and the rum in a bowl. Leave to soften overnight.

Put the egg yolks and castor sugar in a bowl and whisk over a pan of simmering water until pale and creamy. Cool.

Whisk the cream with the mixed spice until thick. Fold in the cold egg yolk mixture, the nuts, chopped fruits and the fruit softened in the rum mixture and all the liquid.

Whisk the egg whites until stiff, then fold into the cream mixture. Turn into a pudding basin that has been lined at the bottom with a piece of greaseproof paper. Cover and freeze until ready to serve.

To serve, quickly dip the pudding basin in hot water to loosen the sides and turn out onto a plate. Serve with Spicy, Island Honey Sauce. Serves 6 – 8.

Spicy, Island Honey Sauce

Like wine and cheese, the flavour of honey varies depending on where it comes from. The unique flavour of Isle of Wight honey is due to the vast maze of hedgerows that twist and turn around the arable and pasture land.

4 tbsp honey
1 tspn mixed spice
1 tbsp chopped walnuts
1 oz (25 gm) butter
¼ pt (150 ml) double cream

Put all the ingredients in a saucepan and simmer gently for 5 minutes, increase the heat and boil for 10 minutes. Serve while hot with the Christmas ice-cream. The combination of hot and cold is divine.

The Glanville Fritillary

The Isle of Wight is a rich haven for tea-rooms, tea gardens and cafes. Many offer their own specialities, whilst others stay true to the traditional British tea and offer simple strawberries and cream, or freshly baked scones with strawberry jam and clotted cream.

Cakes were a great Victorian favourite. Victoria Sandwich, named after the queen, was made for special-occasion tea parties at Osborne House. Traditionally the rich sponge was sandwiched together with raspberry jam.

Victoria Sandwich

4 oz (110 gm) butter
4 oz (110 gm) castor sugar
2 eggs
4 oz (110 gm) self-raising flour
few drops of vanilla essence

Cream together the butter and sugar until soft, pale and fluffy. Beat in the eggs one at a time, adding a teaspoon of flour with each egg if there are signs of curdling. If the butter is soft enough this shouldn't happen. Beat in the vanilla essence. Sift the flour and gently fold into the mixture.

Lightly oil and flour two 6 inch sandwich tins and divide the mixture evenly between both. Level out the mixture then make a small shallow hollow in the centre.

Bake in a preheated oven gas 5/375f/190c for 20-25 minutes. When cooked, turn out and cool on a wire rack. Sandwich together with raspberry jam. These days strawberry or apricot jam or lemon curd are also used and even fresh whipped cream for a more luxurious Victoria Sandwich. Serves 6 – 8.

Cranberry Tart

Queen Victoria's sweet tooth meant that all types of cakes and biscuits had to be freshly baked for her. Sweet confections were often sent over to the Island from her London kitchens to add to the supply.

Cranberry tart was a favourite of hers. I don't have the recipe, but here is a version that I think she may well have tried.

6 oz (175 gm) short sweet crust pastry
4 oz (110 gm) fresh cranberries
3 eggs
4 oz (110 gm) castor sugar
finely grated rind of 1 orange

Line a flan ring with the pastry and bake blind gas 7/425f/ 220c for 10 minutes.

Beat the eggs and mix with the cranberries, orange rind and sugar. Pour into the pastry case and bake gas 4/350f/190c for 40-45 minutes or until the filling is set. When cool sprinkle with icing sugar.

Rose Petal and Peach Cake

4 large eggs
4 oz (110 gm) flour
4 oz (110 gm) castor sugar
1 tbsp rosewater
2 or 3 ripe peaches, blanched in hot water
and skins removed
8 oz (225 gm) icing sugar
4 oz (110 gm) butter
4 oz (110 gm) cream cheese

Place the eggs, castor sugar and rosewater in a large bowl over a saucepan of rapidly simmering water. (Don't allow the bowl to touch the water). Whisk, preferably with an electric whisk, until the mixture is very thick and fluffy. When the whisk is lifted you should be able to draw a figure of eight that will lay on top of the mixture. Sift the flour twice. Wait until the egg mixture is cold, then very gently, so as not to deflate the air, fold in the flour. When thoroughly mixed, divide the mixture between two 7-8 inch, fairly deep sponge tins, that have been lightly oiled and floured.

Bake in a preheated oven gas 4/350f/180c for 20-30 minutes or until the sponges are golden and are beginning to shrink from the sides of the tin. Turn out immediately and cool.

Beat together the sifted icing sugar, butter and cream cheese. Dice half of the peaches and mix into 2/3 of this icing and use to sandwich the sponge together.

Spread the remaining icing on top of the sponge and decorate with the rest of the peaches cut into slices.

In the 13th century the fertile Isle of Wight was a prolific supplier of corn, some of which was transported by ship to Scotland to feed the soldiers fighting for Edward I against the Scots. By the time the three month voyage to Berwick was over much of the corn had gone mouldy. Further supplies were lost when winter sailings proved treacherous and several ships sank.

In the 1790's the Island became a major supplier of wheat and barley to the south of England. The enthusiasm for wheat production in such quantities was generated by the 'No Taxes' law, which greatly increased the wealth of the Island farmers.

After a slump in the mid-19th century farming on the same scale was never resurrected. Many farms were sold up and those that remained turned to milk production.

The First World War brought about a shortage of foreign imports and the Islanders were encouraged to produce their own food. Market gardening quickly got under way and a large variety of seasonal crops were produced.

There are still several water-powered corn mills on the Island – mainly relics of the past – and Millers Damsel at Calbourne continues to produce its own stone-ground flour. It has a wonderful nutty flavour and makes the most delicious wholemeal bread.

Wholemeal Bread

2 lb (900 gm) Calbourne Mill wholemeal flour
1 lb (450 gm) strong white flour
1 level tbsp salt
¼ pt (150 ml) buttermilk
1 sachet easy yeast
30 fl oz (900 ml) tepid water (the absorbency of wholemeal
flour varies therefore you may need a little more
or a little less water)

Mix together the two flours, salt and yeast in a large bowl. Make a well in the centre and pour in the buttermilk and most of the water. Stir to a stiff dough.

Turn out onto a lightly floured board and knead for 2 minutes. Put back in the bowl and cover with a damp tea towel. Place in a warmish place (not hot) to rise for 1 hour.

Knead the bread again for 2 minutes then divide between three 1 lb loaf tins. Put back in a warm place to rise. You could leave the bread in a cold place, it will still rise but will take longer.

When the loaves have risen to double their size, bake in a preheated (this is important) oven gas 8/450f/230c for 35-40 minutes. Turn out of the tin immediately and cool on a wire rack.

Apple and Cinnamon Scones

8 oz (225 gm) plain flour
1 tspn baking powder
1 large eating apple
pinch of salt
1 level tspn cinnamon
1 oz (25 gm) castor sugar
2 tbsp olive oil
7 fl oz (200 ml) buttermilk or milk

Sift together the flour, baking powder, salt, cinnamon and sugar. Peel and core the apple and cut into small dice. Heat the oil in a frying pan and cook the apples gently until tender. Add the apples with the oil to the flour then stir in the buttermilk. Mix to a stiff dough being careful not to overwork the mixture. Roll out to about ½ inch thick and cut circles with a 2 inch cutter. Place on a lightly oiled baking tray and bake in a preheated oven gas 7/425f/220c for 15 minutes. When cooked cool on a wire rack.

Surprisingly, the Isle of Wight is famous for its dough-nuts, and not so long ago it seemed every baker had his own special recipe, including ones filled with jam, cur-rants, apples or cream. Some are squidgy and stretchy, others plump and doughy; some covered in icing, others in spicy sugar. Only recently I spied banana doughnuts at Mapes bakery in Sandown.

The origins of the Isle of Wight doughnut are unknown, but traditionally they contained dried fruit rather than jam: and of course they would have been cooked in lard. There is a recipe for 'Isle of Wight dough-nuts' in the 1845 edition of *Modern Cookery for Private Families* by Eliza Acton, and another recipe in the Isle of Wight W.I. cook book, which because of its huge quantities must have come from a local bakery.

Currant Doughnuts

12 oz (350 gm) strong flour
2 oz (50 gm) butter, 1 packet quick yeast
1½ oz (40 gm) sugar, 4 tspn dried nutmeg
1 egg, 3 oz (75 gm) raisins
1 oz (25 gm) candied peel, 2 fl oz (50 ml) milk
oil for deep frying (or to be truly traditional use lard)
4 tbsp fine castor sugar mixed with 1 tspn
cinnamon for dredging

Rub the butter into the flour. Add the yeast, sugar, nut-meg, raisins and candied peel. Add the milk and beaten egg. If the mixture is too dry add a tiny drop more milk. Mix to a dough and knead until smooth and elastic.

Put the dough in a bowl, cover with a damp cloth then stand in a warm place for a couple of hours until risen.

Knead again and then divide into small balls the size of tangerines. If there is any fruit protruding on the outside of the dough push it into the mix, so that they don't burn when deep fried.

Heat oil or lard in a deep pan to a temperature of 165c/325f. Cooking a few at a time, deep fry until they have turned a golden brown on both sides. Turn over if necessary. Remove from the oil and while still hot dredge in the cinnamon sugar.

Almond Slice

This popular tea-room treat reflects the abundant use of almond flavouring in the 19th century.

4 oz (110 gm) flour
2½ oz (70 gm) butter
1 oz (25 gm) icing sugar
½ small beaten egg
2 tbsp raspberry or strawberry jam
4 oz (110 gm) ground almonds
6 oz (175 gm) castor sugar
2 tspn plain flour, 2 egg whites
1 drop almond essence

Rub the butter into the 4 oz (110 gm) flour. Add the icing sugar and the beaten egg and draw together into a ball. Put in the fridge to rest for 30 minutes. Roll out the pastry and line a small oblong flan tin. Spread over the jam.

Mix together the ground almonds, sugar and flour. Add the egg whites and almond essence and beat well. Pour over the jam and spread to the sides.

Bake in a preheated oven gas 7/425f/220c for 15 minutes. Then lower the heat to gas 4/350f/180c and cook for a further 25 minutes. Cool, then cut into slices.

Apricot Crumble Tart

Serve this sweet warm with vanilla ice cream.

6 oz (175 gm) sweet short crust pastry made with: 6 oz (175 gm) flour, 3½ oz (90 gm) butter, 1 oz (25 gm) icing sugar, 1 egg yolk.

8 oz (225 gm) dried apricots
juice and grated rind of 1 orange
4 oz (110 gm) flour
3 oz (75 gm) demerara sugar
4 oz (110 gm) butter
4 oz (110 gm) coarse oatmeal

Chop up the apricots and put in a saucepan with the orange juice and rind and ½ pt (275 ml) water. Simmer gently until the apricots have become a pulp. Cool slightly.

Roughly rub together the flour and butter. (Keep the mixture fairly lumpy). Stir in the sugar and oatmeal.

Roll out the pastry and line a 10 inch flan ring. Spread over the apricot purée then sprinkle over the crumble mixture. Press down lightly. Bake in a preheated oven gas 7/425f/220c for 40 minutes. Serves 6 – 8.

Ginger Meringues

The mystery of achieving perfect meringues is in the oven. Temperatures vary tremendously from one oven to the next and it is essential to discover how accurate yours is before you can master perfect meringues. Other factors also play a part; egg size, the quantity of sugar, how long you have beaten the meringues for, even the weather. Small individual meringues tend to be easier to handle than large pavlovas, so why not cheat? Make lots of small ones and pile them up as you would profiteroles.

4 egg whites
8 oz (225 gm) castor sugar
2 heaped tspn ground ginger
½ pt (275 ml) double cream

Divide the sugar in half. To one half mix in the ground ginger. Beat the egg white in a clean bowl until stiff. Whisk in the plain sugar until the meringue feels firm to the touch. Lightly whisk or fold in the ginger-flavoured sugar.

Line a baking sheet with tin foil and lightly oil. Spoon or pipe meringue shapes on this baking sheet. Put in an oven that has been preheated to gas 2/300f/140c. Lower heat immediately to gas 1/275f/140c for approx 1 hour, maybe longer, until the meringues are dry.

When cold sandwich together with whipped cream and if wished garnish with crystalized ginger. Serves 4.

Calbourne Classic Clotted Cream Fudge Tart

6 oz (175 gm) sweet short crust pastry made with:
6 oz (175 gm) flour, 3½ oz (90 gm) butter,
1 oz (25 gm) icing sugar, 1 egg yolk

8 oz (225 gm) demerara sugar
½ pt (275 ml) or 8 oz (225 gm) clotted cream
1 oz (25 gm) butter
1 tspn vanilla essence
2 oz (50 gm) glace cherries
4 oz (110 gm) hazelnuts, roughly chopped

Roll out the pastry and line a 6-7 inch flan ring. Bake blind until a pale golden colour. In a heavy bottomed saucepan put the clotted cream, butter, sugar and vanilla essence. Heat gently without boiling, stirring until the sugar has dissolved. Now boil steadily stirring occasionally, until the mixture reaches a temperature of 215f/102c on a sugar thermometer. Remove from the heat and beat in the cherries and nuts. Pour into the baked pastry case and cool until set. Serve with whipped cream.

The Isle of Wight is blessed with numerous tea-rooms, which as well as providing the excuse for a glorious home-made tea offer a chance to get out and explore its quieter backwaters and small villages. The recipes are ones I have picked up on my 'afternoon tea' jaunts around the Island. The ideas are theirs, the recipes my own interpretation.

Jireh House Spicy Fruit Scones

Jireh House Tea Rooms in Yarmouth has now been recommended in the *Just a Bite* guide for several years. It's almost impossible to resist their scones with strawberry jam and thick clotted cream.

8 oz (225 gm) plain flour
1 tspn baking powder
pinch of salt
pinch of sugar
3 oz (75 gm) mixed dried fruit
1 heaped tspn mixed spice
7 fl oz buttermilk or milk
1 small beaten egg

Mix together all the dry ingredients making sure they are thoroughly blended.

Mix the egg with the buttermilk then add to the dry ingredients. Mix lightly together to a stiff but loose dough. Roll out to about ½ inch thick and cut circles with a 2 inch pastry cutter. Place on a lightly oiled baking tray and bake in a preheated oven gas 7/425f/220c for 15 minutes.

When cooked cool on a wire rack. Serve with strawberry jam and Calbourne Classics clotted cream.

Sparkle Cake

A favourite of the End of The Line Tea Rooms at Afton Garden Centre, Freshwater, and incredibly self-indulgent; only small slices should be served!

6 oz (175 gm) multi-coloured glace cherries
6 oz (175 gm) mixed whole nuts
4 tbsp golden syrup
1 tbsp molasses sugar
2 large eggs
4 oz (110 gm) self-raising flour
4 oz (110 gm) butter
4 oz (110 gm) castor sugar
few drops almond essence

Lightly oil and flour a 4 inch deep, 7-8 inch wide cake tin. Into the bottom of the tin put the golden syrup. Scatter the glace cherries and nuts over the syrup and then the molasses sugar.

Cream together the butter and sugar until light and fluffy. Add the beaten eggs, beating thoroughly with a small amount of the flour if there are signs of curdling. Whisk in the almond essence. Lightly fold in the previously sifted flour.

Spread the sponge mix over the fruit and nuts. Bake in a preheated oven gas 5/400f/190c for 45-50 minutes. Test with a skewer. If it comes out clean the sponge is baked.

Cool slightly in the tin before turning out. Turn out so that the bottom is on the top. Serve cold.

Banana Sponge Cake

At the Gallery Cafe, Beavis Store, Newport, Mavis's speciality is homemade cakes. This is, for my taste, one of her best.

3 eggs
6 oz (175 gm) butter
6 oz (175 gm) sponge flour
6 oz (175 gm) castor sugar
2 ripe bananas

Filling
1 firm banana
8 oz (225 gm) icing sugar
4 oz (110 gm) butter
4 oz (110 gm) cream cheese
1 tbsp lemon juice

Cream together the butter and castor sugar until light and fluffy. Beat in the eggs adding a small amount of flour if there is any sign of curdling. Mash the bananas to a soft pulp and beat into the mixture. Sift the flour and fold into the creamed mixture. Divide the mixture between two lightly oiled and floured sponge tins. Bake in a preheated oven gas 5/375f/190c for 25-30 minutes until golden and firm. Cool slightly before turning out.

For the filling, mash the banana with the lemon juice. Cream with the butter, cream cheese and icing sugar. Beat until light and fluffy. Sandwich the sponge cakes together with half the filling and spread the rest on top.

Lemon Rock Buns

From Gods Providence House, St Thomas Square, Newport.

8 oz (225 gm) self-raising flour
4 oz (110 gm) butter or margarine
6 oz (175 gm) granulated sugar
finely grated rind of 2 lemons
pinch of salt
3 eggs
glacé cherries for the tops

Rub the butter into the flour to form fine breadcrumbs. Stir in the sugar and pinch of salt. Add the lemon rind and the beaten eggs. Mix to a stiffish paste. If too stiff add a drop of milk (not too much, if the mixture is too soft the buns will spread out and become flat). Place spoonfuls of the mixture on a baking tray allowing spaces in between for spreading. Top each bun with half a glacé cherry.

Bake in a preheated oven gas 5/375f/190c for 25-35 minutes, until a pale brown and cooked throughout.

Newport's Blue Jenny

Little Pots of Chocolate

From the highly acclaimed Seaview Hotel, Seaview.

10 oz (275 gm) plain Bournville or darker chocolate
1 pt (570 ml) single cream
1 oz (25 gm) castor sugar (optional)
3 tbsp dark rum or coarse brandy
1 sachet of gelatine (1 level teaspoon removed)
1 oz (25 gm) butter

Melt the chocolate in a basin over a saucepan of simmering water. Be very careful not to let any moisture touch the chocolate.

Put the cream and sugar in a saucepan and sprinkle over the gelatine. Stand for a couple of minutes until the gelatine has swollen. Heat gently until the gelatine has melted and the sugar dissolved. Add the melted chocolate to the cream and stir thoroughly. Take off the heat and add the rum. Pour into ramekin dishes or pretty cups. Cool, then chill in the refrigerator. Serve with a dollop of whipped cream and a sweet strawberry. Makes about 6.

JAMS, CHUTNEYS AND DRINKS

Strawberry and Elderflower Jam

An exquisite marriage of flavours, just in time for the first crop of strawberries.

6 lb (2.8 kg) strawberries
juice of 2 lemons
6 lb (2.8 kg) preserving sugar
12 heads of elderflowers gathered just as the umbles
have freshly opened

Wash and hull the strawberries. Layer the strawberries and sugar in a preserving pan, cover and leave to stand overnight.

Next day add the lemon juice and bring the contents of the pan slowly to the boil. Boil for 5 minutes then add the washed elderflowers. Boil for a further 20 minutes or until setting point has been reached. Don't forget to take the pan off the boil while testing for setting point. Alternatively boil using a sugar thermometer until the temperature has reached 220f/103c.

Sterilize the jam jars by heating in the oven. Remove the clusters of elderflowers from the jam with a fork and while the jam is still hot, pour into the jam jars and seal immediately.

Japonica Conserve

Although it is difficult to get hold of quince fruits this preserve can still be made with the fruits from the Japonica Chaenomeles shrub. Because its fruit hasn't been 'domesticated' so to speak, there are quite a lot of pips and peel relative to the amount of flesh. You will need a lot of fruit to obtain enough pulp.

Japonica preserve has a distinctly unique taste. Because of this I tend to use it with other flavours; for example as an addition to apple pies or baked souffles.

2 lb (900 gm) japonica fruits (Japanese quince)
juice of 2 lemons
preserving sugar measured according to the
amount of pulp

Cut the quinces in half. Put in a preserving pan and just cover with water. Simmer until the fruit is soft. Push the fruit through a sieve or mouli mill to remove the pips and peel.

Measure the purée in a measuring jug and weigh out 1 lb (450 gm) sugar to 1 pt (570 ml) fruit purée.

Put the fruit purée and sugar in a preserving pan and stir over a gentle heat until the sugar has dissolved. Bring to the boil and boil rapidly until setting point is reached. Don't forget to remove the pan from the heat when testing for set.

Sterilise jam jars by heating them in the oven, then pour the preserve in the pots while still hot.

Apple and Herb Jelly

To preserve that wonderful taste of summer the British created a tradition we can be proud of. There are numerous recipes old and new for conserving sudden gluts of food.

5 lb (2.3 kg) tart cooking apples or windfalls
2 pt (1.2 lt) water
4 or 5 sprigs of fresh herbs (mint, sage, rosemary)
½ pt (275 ml) white wine vinegar
preserving sugar
8 tbsp finely chopped herbs (pick the new seasons tender
growth particularly in the case of rosemary)

Chop the apples and place in a preserving pan with the water and sprigs of herbs. Bring to the boil and simmer for 45 minutes or until pulpy. Add the vinegar and boil for a further 5 minutes. Set up a jelly bag and strain the pulp overnight. Be patient and don't be tempted to squeeze the bag or the fruit juice will become cloudy.

Measure the clear juice and put into a clean preserving pan with 1 lb (550 gm) of sugar per 1 pt (570 ml) of juice. Stir over a gentle heat until the sugar has dissolved, then boil rapidly for 10-15 minutes or until setting point is reached.

Remove from the heat. Skim the surface then add the chopped herbs. Cool slightly, then stir again to distribute the herbs evenly. Pour while still warm into sterilised jars that have been heated in the oven. Seal immediately.

Garlic and Honey Jelly

2 lb (900 gm) tart windfall apples
1 bulb of garlic
2 tbsp white wine vinegar
1 lb (450 gm) jar of honey
sugar
¾ pt (450 ml) water

Chop the apples and put in a preserving pan with the water. Bring to the boil and simmer for 45 minutes or until pulpy. Add the vinegar and boil for a further 5 minutes. Set up a jelly bag and strain the pulp overnight. Be patient and don't be tempted to squeeze the bag or the fruit juice will become cloudy.

Measure the clear juice and put into a clean preserving pan with 8 oz (225 gm) of sugar per 1 pt (570 ml) of juice and the honey. Stir over a gentle heat until the sugar has dissolved, then boil rapidly for 10 minutes. Break up the bulb of garlic, remove all the papery skins and finely chop. Add to the apple and honey jelly and boil for a further 5 minutes or until the jelly has reached setting point. Remove from the heat. Cool slightly, then stir again to distribute the chopped garlic evenly. Pour while still warm into sterilised jars that have been heated in the oven. Seal immediately.

Elderberry and Crab Apple Chutney

Both these fruits ripen at the same time, and the wood-lands of the Island are brimming with both during the autumn months.

8 oz (225 gm) chopped onions
1 pt (570 ml) red wine vinegar
1 ½ lb (700 gm) crab apples, cored and sliced
1 ½ lb (700 gm) elderberries, stripped from their stalks
8 oz (225 gm) sultanas
1 red chilli pepper, deseeded and sliced
1 tspn ground ginger
1 tspn ground allspice
1 tspn ground cinnamon
1 tspn cayenne pepper
2 oz (50 gm) salt
8 oz (225 gm) sugar

Simmer the onions in some water for about 5 minutes until tender. Strain. Put the onions back in the preserving pan with a third of the vinegar and the rest of the ingredients except the sugar. Simmer until the juice from the elder-berries has been drawn out and the mixture has thickened.

Add the rest of the vinegar and the sugar and simmer again until thick. There should be no apparent liquid when a wooden spoon is drawn through the chutney. While still hot, pack the chutney in hot sterile jars that have been heated in the oven.

Autumn Fruit Pickle

1 lb (450 gm) plums, halved and stoned
1 lb (450 gm) windfall or other apples, peeled and cored
1 lb (450 gm) tomatoes, chopped
1 lb (450 gm) onions, finely sliced
1 lb (450 gm) sultanas
2 large cloves of garlic, chopped
1 pt (570 ml) vinegar
½ tspn ground mace
½ tspn ground mixed spice
2 tbsp ground ginger
1 lb (450 gm) demerara sugar

Put all the ingredients except the sugar in a preserving pan. Mix well together, then heat gently and simmer without boiling for about 40 minutes until everything is tender.

Add the sugar and stir until it has dissolved. Simmer (do not boil), stirring occasionally until the pickle is thick and no pools of liquid lie on the surface when depressed with a wooden spoon.

Cool before packing into sterile jars that have been heated in the oven.

Fiery Tomato 'Glut' Pickle

Splendid with curries and strong Cheddar cheese.

10 red chillis, deseeded and finely sliced
2 oz (50 gm) fresh root ginger
2 tspn ground turmeric
6 tspn cumin seeds
½ pt (275 ml) vegetable oil
10 cloves of garlic, skinned and crushed
8 oz (225 gm) sugar
2 tbsp salt
½ pt (275 ml) vinegar
4 lb (1.8 kg) ripe but firm tomatoes

Grind together the chillis, root ginger, turmeric and cumin seeds in a little oil. Heat the rest of the oil in a preserving pan. Add the ground spices and fry for 1-2 minutes. Reduce the heat and add the garlic, sugar, salt and vinegar. Stir together. When the sugar has dissolved add the tomatoes and cook until pulpy and there is no residue of liquid. Check seasoning, add more salt if necessary.

Leave to cool then pack into sterile jars that have been heated in the oven. Seal.

Pickled Mushrooms

Pickled mushrooms make a good hors d'oeuvre, and are excellent with pâté and cold chicken.

3 lb (1.4 kg) mushrooms, 2 tbsp sea salt
1 pt (570 ml) red wine vinegar
½ pt (275 ml) red wine
2 inch piece of bruised root ginger, 6 cloves

Wipe the mushrooms clean (keep them dry), and put them in a deep bowl. Sprinkle with the salt and leave overnight, covered with a cloth.

Simmer in their own juices until all the liquid has been absorbed. Add the vinegar, wine, ginger and cloves. Bring to the boil and cook steadily for 10 minutes. Leave to cool before bottling in sterile jars. If you are going to use them often keep in an enclosed container in the fridge.

Wild Blackberry Cordial

2 lb (900 gm) blackberries
1 lb (450 gm) granulated sugar
¼ whole nutmeg
cinnamon stick
½ pt (275 ml) brandy

Wash and hull the blackberries. Puree the fruit in a processor and sieve. Put the purée in a preserving pan with the sugar and spices. Heat gently, stirring until the sugar has dissolved. Cover and simmer for 15 minutes. Cool slightly then add the brandy. (If you add the brandy to a hot mixture some of the alcohol will be lost).

Using a funnel pour into sterile bottles that have been heated in the oven. Serve as a liqueur at Christmas.

Sloe Gin

Yet another hedgerow fruit that is abundant along the verges of the Island's country lanes. The fruit are ready to pick in November after the first frosts, when they have developed a deep bluish-black colour with a soft delicate bloom. They contain a great deal of tannin, which gives them their sour taste; hence most recipes containing sloes require more sugar than usual.

Weights will depend on the size of your kilner jar.

sloes, castor sugar
gin, almond essence

Wipe the sloes clean and prick them with a needle. Estimate the amount of sloes you need to half fill your kilner jar and weigh the same amount of castor sugar. Put both the sugar and the sloes in the jar. Fill the jar to the top with the gin and screw the lid on tightly.

Over the next few weeks, shake the jar and turn it upside down regularly. Take off the lid and add a few drops of almond essence. Tightly re-seal and leave in a warm place for 10 weeks, shaking occasionally. Strain through a jelly bag before bottling.

The Needles

INDEX